BRITAIN'S INSPIRATIONAL GARDENS

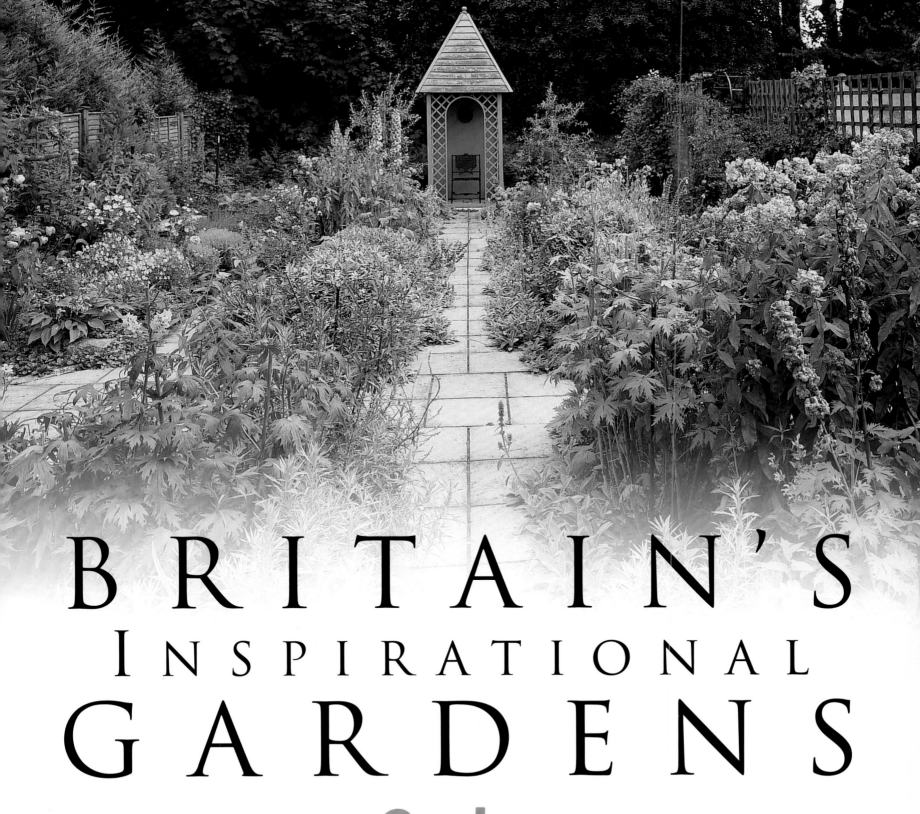

BRITAIN'S
INSPIRATIONAL
GARDENS

Garden answers
MAGAZINE

Materials © Emap Active Limited 2004
Compilation and cover design © Haynes Publishing 2004

All rights reserved. No part of this publication may be reproduced, stored in a retrieval system or transmitted, in any form or by any means, electronic, mechanical, photocopying,
recording or otherwise, without prior permission in writing from the publisher.

First published in 2004

A catalogue record for this book is available from the British Library

ISBN 1 84425 161 6

Published jointly by
Haynes Publishing, Sparkford,
Yeovil, Somerset BA22 7JJ, England
Phone 01963 440635, www.haynes.co.uk
And
Emap Active Limited,
Wentworth House, Wentworth Street,
Peterborough PE1 1DS, England
Phone 01733 213700, www.emap.com

Printed and bound in England by J.H. Haynes & Co. Ltd, Sparkford

CONTENTS

Foreword

by Nicola Dela-Croix

Editor - *Garden Answers*

Whatever your level of gardening experience, it's never too early, or too late, to be inspired by other people's green-fingered efforts. Which is why *Garden Answers* has put together a collection of 26 Inspirational Gardens. As well as being lovely to look at, these gardens will give you plenty of ideas for everything from planting combinations and border shapes, to container collections and patio designs. Each proud owner reveals how the garden was created, together with their tips for planting success. So put down your trowel and enjoy a private tour of some of Britain's most gorgeous gardens.

The publishers would like to acknowledge the diligent efforts of Susan Voss and the staff of Emap Licensing for making this project possible.

The Secret Garden

This Norfolk garden has hidden corners that delight the senses with their planting treasures.

An enticing view, looking past the gazebo down herbaceous borders to *Kolkwitzia amabilis* (beauty bush), which has bushy, pale-pink flowers

Beetroot is an easy crop to grow and a favourite in David and Brian's garden

What are the ingredients of the perfect garden? We'd all have a different reply, but this cottage garden, created by David King and Brian Ellis, comes fairly close in Garden Answers' view. It's not just the exquisite mix of plants, but the fact that they have combined the best of everything. Tantalising corners filled with horticultural treasures, and delicious fruit and veg that are just bursting at the seams with goodness. All these elements are bounded by a wide sweep of lawn which leads your eye through the garden and off to the glorious meadows beyond.

It hasn't always looked perfect, however! David and Brian bought the 17th century cottage in Norfolk 19 years ago, and the garden was a jungle of weeds. 'There were millions of them,' recalls David. 'The previous owners had renovated the house, then simply ploughed through the whole of the garden with a rotavator. In doing so, I should think they multiplied all the weeds a thousandfold...'

Clematis 'Sunset' and the yellow-leaved jasmine 'Fiona Sunrise' are decorative companions on a garden archway

Weeding the quarter-acre plot – at weekends only – was slow progress. 'I started off in one corner trying to weed and dig it over,' explains David. 'And after a weekend when I'd completed a patch about four feet square I thought, My God, what have we let ourselves in for?'

David was still living and working in Barnet, north London, where he kept an allotment. His expertise with home-grown fruit and veg came in handy when keeping weeds at bay. 'Growing crops of potatoes was the only way to keep the soil clear,' he explains. 'Then we just kept it going, moving the vegetable plot around the garden as we cleared more space.'

David was adamant that nothing else was planted until the ground was totally clear – seven years later! Then, finally, they started to lay the garden out, creating a permanent kitchen garden, a number of small borders, and seeding a large area in the middle to create a lawn.

Plant French beans and you're almost guaranteed a bumper harvest

Their patience, hard work and determination soon began to pay off so that now David's neat rows of onions, parsnips and potatoes look - and taste - delicious, anchoring the garden firmly to its cottage garden roots and giving it a practical purpose as well as ornamental and sensual appeal.

In contrast, Brian is the plantaholic of the partnership, taking responsibility for all the ornamental planting - including an 80-strong collection of sempervivums (house leeks)... 'They're gorgeous to look at close up and are fairly easy-care. All they require is just a little weeding.'

Another of Brian's cottage garden favourites is the little annual *Verbascum phoeniceum*, which blooms in shades of white and pale pink through to violet and purple, and pops up again and again throughout the garden.

'I think it's a very underrated plant,' he says. 'We started off with a packet and let them seed every year – they're very promiscuous and produce lots of different colours.'

ROOMS AND VISTAS

'For me, the whole point of gardening is to make rooms and vistas,' says Brian. 'We 'borrowed' our vista over the fields next door, which you can see from the kitchen window, and then created secret places.'

One such 'secret place' is David's vegetable garden. This is hidden away behind a barrier of gorgeous shrubs – magnolia, weigela, holly and kolkwitzia, which are in turn underplanted on one side by annual verbascums, foxgloves, and spiky *Sisyrinchium striatum* and on the other by aquilegias and the daisy-like heads of *Tanacetum coccineum*. The outer perimeter is lined with soft fruit to help it blend visually into the bramble-filled hedgerows of the adjacent field. Indeed, David's most successful fruit crop last year was autumn-fruiting raspberries, which, he says, produce a much higher yield than the summer-fruiting varieties, and are flushed with succulent berries from mid-August right through to mid-November.

Another secluded area is tucked away behind long, flowing borders filled with tall perennials. Its entrance is framed by a gazebo and once inside you're greeted by a green haven of manicured lawn with a close-cropped hedge of *Lonicera nitida*, a shrubby honeysuckle. Nearby, the walls of the garage are becoming obscured by wisteria, clematis and passion flower.

Finally, just 18 months ago, a gravel garden next to the house was landscaped with archways, trellis, a water feature and yet more flower borders. But when it came to edging those borders David hit a frustrating obstacle, quite literally. 'About 17.5cm (7in) down I hit a solid concrete pad - probably the footings of an old shed. I was gobsmacked. I had to chop my way through the concrete where I needed the posts to go, using a hammer and chisel...'

Top: The large starry heads of *allium* 'Globemaster' (AGM) are popular with insects, especially bees

Bottom: Contrasting with the herbaceous borders, the kitchen garden is laid out in neat rows, with onions, parsnip, carrots, beetroot and potatoes

David and Brian's Garden

How long has it taken?
About 14 years. We first started planting in late 1984 when we re-seeded the lawn from scratch. It worked out a lot cheaper than turf

How large is the garden? A quarter of an acre. It faces south-east, fortunately!

Why did you choose these flowers? With the more unusual ones, it's because of their names! I love *Michauxia tchihatchewii!* Also I like the sound of dictamnus and *Zigadenus elegans*

Why did you choose the veg? Because they're the ones we like eating! We're both keen chefs and love to just walk out into the garden, pick, cook and eat our own fresh food within the hour

What are your favourite plants?
We love fritillaries, lilies and also sempervivums - we've got 60 to 80 of them lined up in pots

Any weeds left? American cress is a pain, but at least we only have to tackle it occasionally

How much time does it take to keep it looking this good? We spend at least four days a week out here in spring and summer. But we enjoy it

Who does all the donkey work?
David. He helps me [Brian] with the heavy stuff, digging the borders

Before: nice mud!

Pick of the plants

1 Verbascums grow well in poor soils as long as they're in a sunny site. If the soil's too rich they become leggy and need support

2 Vibrant climber, *Lonicera tellmanniana (AGM)* reaches 5m (15ft) in height with copper, orange and yellow flowers

3 *Anchusa azurea* 'Loddon Royalist' (AGM) is a perennial variety of alkanet with deep blue flowers. H90cm (3ft)

4 The striking stems of marestail, *Equisetum hyemale affine*. Grow in pots to limit its spread

5 Add late summer colour with clematis 'Gravetye Beauty'. It looks spectacular growing up an obelisk

6 The foxglove 'Dwarf Temple Bells' reaches only 30cm (1ft) in height and is a lovely choice near the front of the border.

A family apple tree shades the Welsh poppy *Meconopsis cambrica*, dwarf foxglove 'Temple Bells' and the grass *Stipa tenuissima* while providing fruit for their table

'The air was blue for days!' laughs Brian. The next big project is to make another island border. 'It's mainly to give us somewhere to put some of the plants that we keep buying,' admits Brian. 'We've got thousands in pots waiting to be planted, and have to water them daily in summer.

'I retired early through ill health,' he adds, 'but now I don't know how I ever had time to go to work!'

Our garden was a stack of rubble...

. . . but now the borders seethe with flowers and alpine plants. We met a couple who had to dig through four inches of farmyard rubble to create an immensely varied cottage garden

'We don't buy each other birthday and Christmas presents any more. We just buy stone troughs,' laughs Joan

It's not all blousy 18th century blooms in the Curtis cottage garden: among the profusion of pastels, Cliff tends his alpine collection, adding an exotic spiky twist

Cliff and Joan Curtis have their own recipe for the perfect cottage garden – take one old farmyard and a smattering of outbuildings, dress liberally with plants and add personality, hard work and love. Tend for 30 years and – voilà! – your garden is done... well almost.

'I'd hate to think that my garden was finished because then what would I do?' asks Joan. 'We're always experimenting with plants and moving things so there's always something on the go.'

Joan and husband Cliff developed their garden in Hacconby, Lincolnshire, once the children had stopped playing football.

'It used to be an old stackyard for hay and there was nothing here except tons of rubble that had been spread over the soil to stop the tractors sinking into the mud. To plant anything or put in a post you had to get through four inches of rubble before reaching soil,' recalls Joan.

The farm is no longer worked but the timber outbuildings remain. White fantail doves live inside, while the exterior is covered with dozens of ancient enamel hoardings advertising familiar old brands such as Colman's Mustard and Gold Flake tobacco. 'I bought them when the village shop was closed 25 years ago, and used them to cover the cracks in the wood,' recalls Cliff. 'They did a great repair job and really brighten up the place.'

As for the garden, first the couple laid a York flagstone terrace with generous, gravel-filled gaps and clouds of white *Erigeron karvinskianus* daisies, topped by the purple heads of *Allium pulchellum* and the wiry stems of *Verbena bonariensis*. The central paving area gradually gives way to wider gravelled spaces on either side, so you can walk among the flowers

Ferns thrive in this shady 'woodland' corner, alongside hellebores and, in late winter, a drift of snowdrops

Hacconby's heron population keeps a very keen eye on the Curtis fishpond. So far the birds haven't managed to get past the single strand fishing line fence

without trampling them. 'We sourced the gravel locally to fit in with the surroundings,' says Joan. 'Continuity of path surfaces through a garden is vital. Too many different types make it look disjointed.'

It's also important that the plants complement the cottage garden look, but soil conditions mean it's not always possible for the couple to grow what they want. Stretching out their fronds in the shade of the house is a lush group of Shield Ferns (*Polystichum setiferum* and *aculeatum*). 'With all the rubble in the soil, hostas were out of the question, so I've planted the ferns instead,' explains Joan. 'They seem to like the shade and it's like a mini-woodland area, with oriental hellebores underplanted with drifts of snowdrops that look fabulous in winter.'

The house lies at the bottom of a south-facing slope. Uphill from the terrace a gravel path leads past a dense, mounded border planted with a patchwork of ground-hugging plants. There's yellow creeping Jenny (*Lysimachia nummularia*), white deadnettle (*Lamium maculatum*), purple-leaved ajuga and silver snow-in-summer (*Cerastium tomentosum*), with a blanket of seasonal hellebores and campanulas.

Cottage garden favourites grow in abundance too: wine-coloured penstemons, variegated sage, blue Jacob's Ladder (polemonium) and new plants such as *Geranium* 'Rozanne', a prolific blue ground cover plant. In the mix are treasures including a perennial form of quaking grass, *Briza media*, with corn-yellow stems and tear-shaped flowers that dance in the slightest breeze. 'We're trying it here but whether it comes up year after year, we shall just have to wait and see,' says Joan.

Variegated box hedging keeps spice-coloured flowers from spilling onto the path. 'Cliff says the space should be used for vegetables,' says Joan

A set of succulents soak up the sunshine, making themselves very much at home among more traditional cottage garden plants

Throughout the garden, plants are combined with care and attention. 'I give new plants two years in one spot and take notes on how they do. If I think they'd look better elsewhere, I stick a label in to remind me to move them.'

The borders are divided by shrub roses such as the early, bright yellow 'Canary Bird' and *Rosa glauca* with its soft, misty-purple leaves. Each rose is contained within a V-shaped timber frame that holds the long, lax briars up off the ground, freeing up the space at their feet for cranesbills to scramble.

Silver birch trees grow on the boundaries. 'I love the tracery of their branches against the blue winter sky, but they're messy – setting seed everywhere and drying out the garden with their roots,' she warns.

Despite this, Joan has established a hydrangea – a plant that normally likes damper conditions – at the base of one of the birches. 'Before planting it we sunk an old tin bath in the soil which acts as a reservoir for its roots,' she says.

While the cottage plants are Joan's responsibility, the alpines and propagation are Cliff's. 'Most plants propagate easily otherwise you wouldn't be able to buy them,' he reasons. 'If you try you'll be surprised where they'll grow.'

Propagation takes place in an area 18mx12m (60ftx40ft). There are glass-houses, soft fruit and vegetable beds. 'We love to have fruit and veg in season,' adds Joan.

There's also a double flower border with an edging of variegated box which stops flame red *Crocosmia* 'Lucifer', burnished *Achillea* 'Terracotta', red dahlias, asters and zingy yellow *Helenium* 'Golden Youth' spilling out onto the path.

'I call this part of the garden my "happy" bit, as the bright colours always cheer me up when I come around the corner.'

These spicy plants are grouped separately so they won't clash with the softer colour tones. 'I call this part of the garden my "happy" bit, as the bright colours always cheer me up when I come around the corner, although Cliff complains about me taking up space which should be for growing vegetables,' says Joan.

Cliff grows hundreds of different alpines from bright pink rhodohypoxis to mound-forming saxifrages and the miniature cranesbill-lookalike, erodiums. 'We don't buy each other birthday or Christmas presents any more,' laughs Joan. 'We just buy stone troughs.'

My favourite from Cliff's alpine collection is a house leek (sempervivum) that grows in a cracked birdbath. The plant has mounded into a dome and looks like a piece of coral. 'Everyone comments on it but it's how they grow naturally,' Cliff points out.

Beside the birdbath is an informal pond. 'We just like to watch the fish,' says Cliff. The couple manage to keep away the herons by stretching fishing line across the water and attaching the ends to trees on either side with elastic. As the herons come in to land, their wings brush the line and the elastic gives. But because they can't see it, it makes them nervous and they don't come back.

One of the 'heron deterrent' trees is a Bramley. Wrapped around one of its lower branches is a mat and there's a besom broom lodged in its crown. Joan explains, 'I wrapped the mat around that branch because I keep banging my head on it when I'm weeding! The broomstick was given to me by my sister's children when they found out that my birthday was on Hallowe'en. I tell them that I keep it in the tree in case I need to nip off anywhere in a hurry!'

About the witchcraft I'm not so sure. But the garden is pure magic.

OUR FAVOURITE IDEAS TO PINCH

- Let plants mingle and self-sow to create a more 'wild and natural' effect
- Leave gaps between paving stones for self-seeders such as *Verbena bonariensis* and *Erigeron karvinskianus*. They'll break up the harsh line where the patio and border meet
- Group hot-coloured plants separately so they don't clash with the softer, pastel shades of more traditional cottage garden flowers
- Create a lush and shady woodland area with ferns such as polystichum and *Asplenium scolopendrium*.

'We're always experimenting and moving things. I give new plants two years in one spot and take notes on how they do.'

Short of a picket fence and roses round the door? The Curtis cottage garden takes a refreshingly modern twist on the 18th century clichés, using (clockwise from top left) Clive's collection of alpine succulents – more Morroccan spice stall than olde worlde romance; euphorbia – subtle and exotic; rusty wire baskets (strategically placed as weed bins); their thoroughly modern Jack Russell, Sandy; the weird and wonderful house leek, sempervivum, grown in a birdbath; wildlife that coos

Left: Andrew Sankey's front garden is packed with cottage garden favourites

Right: The large red blooms of a rhododendron shine against a carpet of pink geraniums

Summer delights

A cottage garden in the front and a turf maze in the back give some clue to the varied tastes of the enthusiasts who created this colourful organic garden in Lincolnshire

When Andrew and Sheila Sankey moved into School House in Lincolnshire, eight years ago, the quarter-acre garden was the star attraction. At last they had the space they'd always wanted and could begin to create a garden that reflected their tastes and needs – there were three children to consider, as well as two enthusiastic gardeners. Sheila had already taken a horticulture course at college and Andrew had

A formal vista divides the front garden and contrasts with the soft planting scheme of persicaria, alliums and nepeta

Foxgloves self–seed freely, producing offspring in shades of pink and purple

Alliums flower in early summer, leaving attractive seedheads behind them

***Aquilegia* 'Nora Barlow' will self seed anywhere – a classic cottage garden plant**

worked as a graphic designer, so the couple were filled with excitement at the thought of transforming the plain lawns into a cottage-garden delight.

The garden at School House has neutral, free-draining soil, which meant Andrew and Sheila could choose from a wide range of plants, as long as they would cope with dry soil. The south-facing front garden is exceptional in summer. Geraniums, digitalis (foxgloves), astrantia and aquilegia jostle for space around mature trees and rhododendrons, and are allowed to seed wherever the wind may take them. 'We like the cottage garden feel and if something doesn't work we take it out and plant it somewhere more suitable,' says Andrew. There are few signs of unsuccessful planting – the garden brims with co-ordinated colour accentuated by the classic red-brick

old school-house. Straight lines of box hedging divide gravel paths from borders of nepeta (catmint), alliums and persicaria. Plants for the front garden have been chosen for their ability to thrive in sun and well-drained soil. Aquilegias are easily grown from seed and seed of favourite forms can be scattered in late summer, after flowering, for more flowers each year. Alliums are another favourite. They originate from the Mediterranean, making them ideally suited to the conditions in this garden. Andrew's favourite plants are irises as they suit his garden's conditions so well. Bearded varieties thrive in the hot, sun-baked soil of the front garden and the Siberian varieties love the cool, dry shade of the back. The colourful front garden makes it easy to forget that there's still the back garden to visit. At this point Andrew's eyes light

Lilium pyrenaicum **flowers in early summer and will multiply if left to establish**

After flowering, dwarf rhododendrons provide shade for late-flowering lilies

Geraniums have a long flowering period, a relaxed habit and are reliably hardy

Aquilegias thrive in the well-drained soil and dappled shade of the front garden

up: 'We use the front garden for more traditional planting and do the adventurous stuff in the back.' He wasn't joking – the straight lines of the front give way to curved walks and adventurous features. This makes the back garden a pleasure to explore as you're never quite sure what you might stumble across next.

'You've got to have surprise in a garden to keep people interested', enthuses Andrew, just as Sheila's pride and joy presents itself: an enormous turf maze that doubles up as an area to grow on cuttings and as a vegetable garden. Producing hundreds of successful cuttings and plenty of veg, the maze is attractive, productive and practical. 'We've always liked turf mazes and we designed ours using a Celtic symbol,' says Andrew. Planted with onions, asparagus, potatoes and beans, the maze is loved by the whole family. You can pause for a rest on two cleverly-placed seats: one for the morning sun and one for the afternoon means there's always somewhere pleasant to sit, depending on your mood.

The turf maze resembles a traditional Celtic symbol and was made by marking out sand circles on an existing lawn. It took about a week to dig out and only takes 10 minutes to cut. The soil areas are used for veg and for bringing on rooted cuttings

'You've got to have surprises in a garden. Enjoy yourself and don't be afraid to try new ideas'

Cobbled paths are attractive and easy to make. First lay the outline then, working on small areas at a time, use a 5:1 cement mix on a bed of flat sand and press in the stones

Iris sibirica **flowers in early summer and will tolerate a wide range of conditions**

Andrew and Sheila pride themselves on being organic, and believe that a garden will arrive at its own ecological balance if left to its own devices. They credit much of their success to generous additions of well-rotted manure, essential in any garden and vital to add bulk to the thin, sandy soil.

But no garden is without its share of challenges. 'Unfortunately we've got lots of moles,' says Andrew. 'The children won't let me harm them so I end up catching them and driving a few miles down the road to release them!' Eccentric maybe, but it's a certainly a solution that satisfies everyone in the family.

The garden appears complete but, like most gardeners, Sheila and Andrew are not satisfied. 'There are a few things that still need to be done, but everything takes time' says Andrew, dreaming of urns, new trellis and yet more planting combinations. Ironically, these comments come after a period of re-development in the front garden to widen the borders and introduce more cottage garden plants! Andrew sums up his approach: 'Enjoy yourself and don't be afraid to try new ideas.'

Choose iris for flowers every summer

Dainty plicata iris, with their blue-edged flowers, thrive in sunny areas

In the north-facing back garden, Siberian iris thrive, blooming in July

Sun-loving bearded iris are available in colours to match bright or pastel schemes

The blooms of white Siberian iris punctuate shadier areas of the garden

Almost black forms of *Iris chrysographes* are among the darkest of all flowers

In June, the elegant flowers of bearded iris give a brief, but sumptuous, display

Exotic jungle plants in the middle of Thetford's pine forests? Whatever next! Here we have the yellow and green striped leaves of *Phormium* 'Yellow Wave' as well as the red and green stripes of *Phormium* 'Jester'. To the left is spiky *Phoenix canariensis*. Bounty bars are optional

Barry Gayton, jungle–maker

Santon
Downham
B1107
4m N.
Thetford.
01842
765861

Welcome to paradise!

Imagine a tropical haven filled with cacti, cannas, palms and passion flowers... Barry Gayton has brought his childhood fantasy to life – deep in an English pine forest!

Hidden deep in the heart of Britain's largest lowland pine forest, on the Norfolk-Suffolk border, Barry Gayton's Desert World is a truly extraordinary garden. Surrounded on all sides by dense woodland, it enjoys a unique micro-climate that's a frost pocket in winter, but becomes a sheltered haven from the biting East Anglian winds from May to November.

This means that alongside his impressive collections of conifers, alpines, grasses, ferns and perennials, Barry is able to indulge his passion for all things exotic. Cacti, palms, cannas, and passion flowers all thrive here, spending their lives in huge pots left outside during summer and

Impressive *Phoenix canariensis* needs a frost-free place to overwinter

What better way to heighten the sensual exotic planting than with *Passiflora caerulea* 'Amethyst'?

'Growing a garden from scratch is great fun'

crammed into greenhouses over winter. 'They stay out for six or seven months of the year, until the first frost warning,' explains Barry. 'Then I bring them in for protection. It's worth the extra effort – tender perennials are far more interesting than your average garden plants, plus you have the added bonus of an uplift in the garden at the back end of summer, with late-flowering plants such as agapanthus, daturas and cannas.'

Walking around his one-acre garden is like taking a turn through a fantasy land, with unexpected and sometimes startling juxtapositions. For instance, under a *Prunus avium* (cherry tree) amid stonecrops and phlox, you'll find *Phoenix canariensis* (Canary date palm) and a couple of phormiums, a row of cannas and *Brugmansia sanguinea* (also known as datura). Planted along the

garden path in the manner of traditional formal bedding, they combine to create the feel of a colonial outpost in the tropics.

Most bizarre is the Totem Pole garden, an extraordinary combination of desert plants and ethnic artefacts: giant cacti, spiky yuccas, an arresting ball sculpture created by Barry himself, and a carved totem pole, commissioned locally a few years ago.

This part of the garden evolved through Barry's long-standing love of cacti and a desire to see them growing outdoors. 'All plants, even houseplants, grow better in the garden than under glass. They remind me of American deserts, cowboys and Indians!'

Barry is, by his own admission, a plantaholic. As well as tending his own garden single-handedly, he works full-time as head gardener at the public gardens in Thetford.

Enjoying the sun at the front of Barry's clapboard house, lines of cannas stand opposite little pots of sempervivums. Yellow gazanias line the path while cheerful yellow and orange marigolds cascade from the windowsill

CREATE A TROPICAL JUNGLE

Give your garden a tropical makeover with these plants.

1 *Dicksonia* (tree fern)
2 *Musa basjoo* (banana)
3 Cannas
4 Crocosmia
5 Dahlias
6 *Brugmansia* (datura)
7 Yucca
8 Phormium
9 Cordyline
10 Cacti
11 *Fascicularia bicolor*
12 Arum lilies
13 Crinum
14 Ferns
15 *Melianthus major*
16 *Trachycarpus fortunei*

Tender plants, such as tree ferns, bananas, fascicularia, cacti and some cordylines, may need protection over winter.

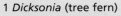

In late autumn, tie up cordylines with string to prevent water entering the centre of the plant. In very cold areas, cover with hessian, fleece or newspaper. Come April, unwrap and start into growth

BARRY'S TIPS FOR GROWING EXOTICS

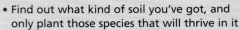

- Find out what kind of soil you've got, and only plant those species that will thrive in it
- If you're growing from seed, try something different. Plant World (tel 01803 872939), Chiltern Seeds (tel 01229 581137) and Plants of Distinction (tel 01449 721720) are among the best
- Grow most of your exotic plants in pots so it's easier to move them indoors over winter. They can then be put out again after the last frosts, around late May
- Cacti require good drainage, especially if grown in pots. Mix grit with the compost when you plant them, never overwater and make sure they get plenty of sunshine
- Don't be frightened of growing something new. Treat it as a challenge and read everything you can about it
- Buy from specialist mail order companies such as Hardy Exotics, tel 01736 740660

**Top: Sow banana plant seeds in moist compost
Right: Cactus spines are very painful so make a paper handle to lift them**

Barry has lived here with his wife, Belinda, and their son, Anthony, for 20 years, in a house completely dominated by plants. In fact, the garden is now so full that three years ago he built a roof garden to accommodate even more! This is Barry's private escape where he can sit and unwind. To help set the relaxing mood, Barry chose rustling bamboos and grasses, plus a mix of sun-worshippers (such as golden hop and *Cerinthe major*) that don't grow too tall, as the area is very exposed.

Barry's passion for plants began when he was a child. 'When I was six, I was given a plot of land at the bottom of the garden, where nothing much would grow,' he laughs. 'I was told to get on with it. It was 10 feet wide by about 50 feet long. I grew seeds and cuttings, but wanted to grow something different, so when most other eight year-old boys were asking for bikes and train sets, I asked my parents for a greenhouse! I got it too – a Silver Mist, which cost £16 and came with a free hamper and turkey! We put it up in the middle of winter, and I sowed my first cactus seed in March.'

Now Barry has more than 13,500 species, including some cacti from that very first sowing. 'I love them for their longevity,' he says. 'Some last a human lifetime. Fuchsias and pelargoniums are over in a year, cacti last forever. Some of mine have only just flowered for the first time after 40 years.'

Barry's latest enthusiasm is for passion flowers, of which he has more than 60 species – from the typically dramatic, deep pink 'Lilac Lady' to the delicate pale apricot of 'Adularia'. Like Barry's other tender plants, these are grown in pots so they can overwinter under cover. As well as protecting them from frost, this ensures the plant doesn't get waterlogged.

All the passion flowers are grown from seed, as are most of the plants in this wonderland. Barry spends time hunting down unusual varieties, and belongs to 19 plant societies so he can swap seed.

'Growing a garden from scratch is great fun,' says Barry. 'Anybody can go and buy a garden, but I've done it on a shoestring here, taking cuttings and sowing seeds. That's the way to do it, because then the garden is full of memories.'

Above: Beloved by bees and gardeners with good taste, *Echinacea purpurea* grows to 1.5m tall, flowering from July through to late October. Just give it sun

Right: The dramatic fans of *Chamaerops humilis* reach 2.5m. It needs a sheltered, sunny position and won't survive heavy frost

Below: Add a little lapis lazuli with jewel-blue agapanthus. These sun-lovers grow to around 1m tall and flower in late summer

'When I was eight, I asked my parents for a greenhouse!'

Our exotic haven

Margaret Hewitt's Staffordshire garden seems traditional English, but a closer look reveals exotic trees and shrubs that give it a strong framework in any season. Find out how she created this paradise garden...

A row of cherry trees provides backbone to Margaret's garden. To the left, *Magnolia soulangeana* is in bloom while on the right, *Liriodendron tulipifera* comes into leaf

PHOTOGRAPHY: BOB ATKINS

"Our trees are planted in island beds and create their own microclimates"

Sixteen years ago I left a beautiful garden full of shrub roses, to come to a 'blank canvas'. Arbour Cottage was a two-acre site with a hedge, large veg plot, one border of annuals and an area of cleared field. But to my husband David and I it was the perfect setting – miles from anywhere and full of potential for creative planting. We bought it as we drove up the lane!

It took five months to sell our old house which gave me ample opportunity to transport lots of plants! I even brought the compost heap!

We garden on sandy soil at Arbour Cottage, so compost-making is vital to enrich the hungry soil. We just can't apply enough compost, which explains the sheer size of some of our trees, which were planted as small 'mop heads'. Our tulip tree, *Liriodendron tulipifera*, is more than 20ft tall and we're eagerly awaiting its first flowers.

Our soil may be sandy, but it's also acid, and so indulges my taste for exotic trees and shrubs from Japan and China. We've planted acers, magnolias, sorbus and ornamental cherries, and these form the backbone of the garden and a strong framework in winter.

Despite being in Staffordshire, we get the garden off to an early start thanks to the trees, which are planted in island beds and create their own microclimates. This provides protection for a mixture of shrubs, roses, clematis and perennials. Tender plants, such as *Cerinthe major* 'Purpurascens', *Geranium maderense* – a bright pink geranium from Madeira – and *Euphorbia mellifera* flourish and are in flower by early May.

I love to see clematis scrambling through trees, and 'Guernsey Cream' – which doesn't need pruning – looks gorgeous against the shiny chestnut-brown trunk of a flowering cherry.

Magnolia brooklynensis 'Yellow Bird' is one of my favourite trees and last year revealed its soft yellow, upright flowers for the first time since planting. Other highlights include our huge pink tree paeony (inset, below), which explodes into flower in midsummer, as well as the dramatic Oriental poppies and billowing euphorbias.

For strong, vertical shapes I love angelicas, thalictrums and kniphofias, all of which contrast well with ferns, hostas and sedges.

Our poor, light soil is also ideal for running plants such as *Euphorbia cyparissias* 'Fens Ruby', a low-growing, feathery plant with wine-coloured leaves

Perfect plants for poor, dry soil

Armeria (thrift)
Dianthus (pinks)
Calendula (pot marigold)
Erysimum (wallflower)
Eschscholzia (Californian poppy)
Kniphofia (red hot poker)
Nigella (love-in-a-mist)
Succulents (agave, aeonium, echeveria)

Margaret's garden

Arbour Cottage, Napley, Market Drayton, Staffordshire
Shares garden with: Husband David
Size of garden: Two acres
Soil type: Poor, dry and sandy
Position: Faces all four points of the compass!
Top tip: Carry on composting! You can't add enough!

Agave americana 'Mediopicta Alba' makes a stunning centrepiece.

and yellow-green flowers. Prevent it rampaging across the garden by thinning it occasionally.

I do allow some plants to seed about freely, without feeling threatened by them! Forget-me-not, carex, Welsh poppies and the bright blue *Geranium pyrenaicum* 'Bill Wallis' seed freely, adding to our cottage garden effect.

If you garden on dry soil, alpines should do well. They thrive in our scree beds where tiny, intricate plants look their best. We mulch with gravel in the sunnier areas and this provides good drainage during damp winters, and a cool root run in summer. It's also a perfect seed bed. Delicate plants are covered with small, bell-shaped glass cloches to protect them from the wet.

We found large boulders of pinkish sandstone when we moved in, which created another natural-look scree bed. We've mulched with grey slate, broken into small slithers, and this tones perfectly with silver celmisias.

During winter our conservatory and greenhouse are packed with giant succulents (agaves, aeoniums and echeverias), until summer, when they're wheeled out onto the terrace. We group five or six similar succulents together to avoid a fussy look. It seems to work, as these plants draw gasps of admiration from visitors!

Halesia carolina is a pretty tree from the United States that flowers in spring. They are followed by attractive, winged seedpods.

Below: *Geranium pyrenaicum* 'Bill Wallis' seeds around freely.

Nestling among rocks in shade, *Polypodium vulgare* is a native fern that tolerates drought once established.

Ornamental cherries add spring freshness before their fallen petals create a snowy carpet.

Magnolia soulangeana thrives in acid soil, benefiting from the shelter of other trees that protect its delicate flowers from cold spring winds.

Sorbus are ideal trees for small gardens – their fine foliage is always attractive and often turns red or orange in winter and the flowers are followed by bright berries.

Willow obelisks make rustic supports that have structure in winter and support the flowering stems of honeysuckle in summer.

With some support from discreet netting, clematis clothe bare tree trunks. The shade benefits pale colours which are less prone to fading.

Centre: An old broken pot makes a comfy home for houseleeks
Bottom centre: The many varieties of *Clematis macropetala* bloom in early spring and are unperturbed by cold winds.

Umbria in Cumbria!

There's a small part of Cumbria that draws its inspiration from the warmth and beauty of Italy. We discover a horticultural hotspot which offers more than just great plants

Yes, this is a nursery. A nicer place to wander and spend money is hard to imagine

The sun's on my face and the aroma of pizza teases my nostrils. I stumble into a Renaissance-style piazza, surrounded by a profusion of hotly-coloured plants, tumble-down walls and elegant Italian-style statuary.

For a moment I'm transported to the Mediterranean... and yet I know that the hum of the M6 motorway is just a few miles away. This is Larch Cottage Nurseries, near Penrith – definitely more Umbria than Cumbria. Breeze through the nursery entrance doors and feast your eyes on a heavenly jumble of pots, statues and urns, birdbaths, ponds, water features and masses of lush greenery.

It's enough to make your head spin, especially on a sunny day. For here, as soon as the sun pops out from behind the Cumbrian clouds to bathe the piazza in dazzling sunlight, you feel as though you've stumbled into a Renaissance Italian garden. Add the aromas of fresh baking and coffee wafting down from the terrace restaurant, and you can soon see why people flock to this nursery from far and wide.

Right: *Geranium oxonianium* 'Walter's Gift' is one of 100 or more hardy geraniums for sale

Above: Mama mia! Even the succulent viburnum berries look sunny and Italian

Opposite: An inviting scene that contains great ideas. Have you got stone steps? Create a feature by placing colourful plants on each step. Instant style!

Right: Nursery owners Briony and Peter Stott with their son, Lucien, amid a melange of all things Umbrian

On the leafy terrace, shaded by a lacy curtain of climbers and hanging baskets, you'll find the perfect place to while away an hour or two. Purely in the interests of research, your reporter settled for a portion of fresh pizza from the restaurant's wood-fired oven, accompanied by a delicious salad! It tasted so good it reminded me of the best pizza I'd ever tasted, somewhere in the back streets of Venice.

This fantasy world is the creation of Peter Stott. Amazingly, when he began building the nursery back in 1985 Peter had never even been to Italy! It wasn't until five years ago, when a teacher friend from the local grammar school suggested he join him on one of his 'art and architecture' tours that our nurseryman got his first vivid taste of Rome. 'I couldn't believe it – I felt like I'd lived there before,' says Peter. 'It was the nearest thing I'd ever had to a feeling of reincarnation.'

Just two weeks later Peter returned to Italy with his wife, Briony, and their three children. The following year he took on a landscape job in Umbria, and the family love affair with Italy had begun.

'My dream is for Larch Cottage Nurseries to be an artistic experience, not just about plants but art and architecture, too. There's no reason why you can't put things in a beautiful context.'

Peter is a local boy and self-confessed workaholic who has at various times been a ballet and modern dancer, tree surgeon and landscape designer. In this last job, he struggled to find the plants he needed nearby, and then the idea of setting up his own nursery sprang to life. Briony gave up her job teaching biology to help and over the years has become an experienced plantswoman. She's especially keen on

perennials and small woodland plants. 'I love anything that blooms in spring,' she smiles. 'Such plants are a joy to behold after a long, cold British winter!'

Larch Cottage Nurseries is a paradise for people interested in plants. And don't be fooled into thinking that because the surroundings are exquisitely Italian, all you'll find here are trendy but impractical plants that need cossetting in winter. Briony and Peter have propagated a range of good, choice, herbaceous plants, most of which are grown on site. There are almost 2000 different kinds, including more than 100 hardy geraniums.

'as the sun lights up the piazza you feel as though you've stumbled into a Renaissance Italian garden'

Peter and Briony are pleased to note how recent mild winters have helped more tender species survive outdoors. Many plants which would have struggled in the north-west 15 years ago now thrive in the climate.

Over the past few years, the Stotts have built up a good range of viburnums and cornus as well as beautiful cercidophyllum. Briony picks out *Cornus mas* for special mention, a rarely seen, totally hardy shrub with a myriad of starry, yellow flowers in spring. Plant the variegated kind and you'll get pretty leaves all summer.

Left: The terrace restaurant. Your largest pizza, please, with extra topping!

Top: Umbria or Japan? Streams and ponds look their best surrounded by lush planting

Elegant urns look suitably grand placed along a walkway

Striking photinia complements *Cornus alba* 'Sibirica Variegata'

Rare and dwarf conifers can be found here too, and though they're not particularly fashionable, they'll be gracing our gardens long after some of the more faddish plants have been turned to compost.

Peter obviously has a flair for architecture, having designed and constructed the nursery's main building himself –

housing the entrance, offices, shop, café and bakery. It makes a bold statement yet doesn't look grandiose or out of place. With its lovely, rambling edifice it manages to grasp the very essence of stylish but crumbling Italy. However, it might have looked very different had the letter of the law been strictly observed!

Despite the building's obvious

'the tumble-down walls are draped in greenery and lit up by multi-coloured stained glass'

Hardly your typical
Lake District scene!

Great shopping opportunities in a beautiful garden. Heaven!

'Steps and stairs

appeal, it didn't conform to local planning regulations and Peter was told to tear it all down within three months!

This order marked the start of a fierce and costly battle with the authorities – Peter estimates he spent £70,000 fighting bureaucracy. Local people supported the Stotts, and eventually common sense prevailed, when an enlightened inspector declared that Peter's design was 'the epitome of vernacular architecture using local materials'. Cue a major street party!

Peter's Umbrian vision has made this not only a distinctive nursery but a great place for a day out. The tumble-down walls are draped in greenery and lit up by glowing stained glass (a technique Peter learned from a monk!). A pergola smothered in climbers provides welcome shade for plants and people alike, while steps and stairs are festooned with pots and containers from which a rainbow of coloured petals spills. There's also the monastic herb garden, along with a large Japanese garden and a piazza which will become an arts centre.

On a sunny day, it's hard to tear yourself away from this haven. I left with a head full of dreams and a car full of plants. Perfection!

are festooned with pots and containers that spill a rainbow of coloured petals'

Above: A monk taught Peter how to make stained glass windows

CREATE YOUR OWN UMBRIAN PARADISE

Treat your garden to a dose of sunny Umbria using these key ingredients.

1 Red pelargoniums – always bright and cheerful on the patio, or trailing from a hanging basket against a white wall. Why not pot up a whole set of them, running up a flight of stone steps?

2 Plant up sun-loving perennials in dusty old terracotta pots. Fluted ones create a more elegant effect.

3 Sow soft, feathery herbs at the front of your borders such as thyme, lavender, myrtle and rosemary; let them brush against your legs as you walk on gravel pathways. Herbs are widely available from garden centres.

4 Invest in cool, classical statuary to smarten up a dull corner. This coquettish statue is named Venus.

5 Pot up small, neat box trees and clip them into bold topiary shapes.

6 Trail plants through a handsome metal urn.

PHOTOGRAPHS: ANNE GREEN-ARMYTAGE

For height among this tapestry of herbs, Janet grows giant grasses *(Stipa gigantea)* and the golden bean tree *(Catalpa bignonioides)*

Herbal instincts

Janet and Maurice Elliotts' Suffolk herb garden is packed with plants for flavour, perfume, potions and lotions – even fabric dyes.

Janet and Maurice Elliott with their dog Sasha, surrounded by petunia 'Priscilla', pansies and rose 'Fragrant Delight'

Have you ever seen a garden packed with herbs? Imagine the fragrance and colour, and you're halfway to experiencing the pleasure of Maurice and Janet Elliott's Suffolk garden. Their third of an acre plot is packed not only with culinary herbs (they have 90 cultivars of mint!) but medicinal plants too. There are herbs for aromatherapy, and a range of natural dyes: woad (blue), madder (turkey red), dyer's woodruff (red), greenweed (yellow), and elderberry (black), hence the elderberry's botanical name, *Sambucus nigra.*

You'd never believe the couple's entry into herb-growing was accidental. Eleven years ago, Maurice's national building business went into

receivership and the couple lost their home, their cars and much of their pension. But with the help of their seven children and a great deal of tenacity, they managed to start again from scratch.

They moved into a dilapidated farm outbuilding (once a medieval hall) and set about restoring it, with Maurice as project manager. At the same time they started to renovate the garden, removing concrete, installing drainage, and digging in tons of leafmould, topsoil and manure.

Janet, finding her budget for plant-buying severely curtailed, had taken cuttings from her former garden, and was soon growing enough to sell as surplus at the local WI market. 'No one was

Purple–blue catmint and yellow coreopsis hug the ankles of the pergola here, framing a view of Janet's heather and conifer collection, all grown from tiny cuttings

Right: In the Elliotts' garden all the flower beds are filled with useful herbs. Here tasty thymes jostle with winter savory *(Satureja montana)* chives and sage

Below: Oil from the evening primrose *(oenethera)* is proven to stimulate hormone-like substances in the body. A Modern Herbal, in 1931 proclaimed the oil could also alleviate 'certain female complaints such as pelvic fullness', too!

Above: Coreopsis 'Sunburst' grows among the herbs, offering flashes of cheerful colour therapy

doing herbs there,' she remembers, 'so I started to specialise, and the business has evolved from there. I didn't set out to start a nursery – I just find it very therapeutic. I go out into my potting shed, and I switch off,' she smiles. 'My children refer to the potting shed as my sheltered accommodation!'

The couple grow many different kinds of herbs in the garden, and feel that, for them, diversity is crucial. 'I only grow a few of a lot rather than a lot of a few,' explains Janet. 'We get the RHS, National Collection Holders, people from Aberdeen, North Wales, even Germany, coming here looking for plants,' adds Maurice. He smiles widely. 'If you want anything odd, try us.'

And they do have some unusual plants. There's spikenard, the herb whose oil was used to anoint the feet of Jesus at the Last Supper. Then there's *Centella asiatica*, the so-called 'arthritis plant' – if you eat a couple of leaves every day, it's said to clear the blood of impurities and help ward off arthritis. And there's even *Spilanthes acmella*, or 'toothache plant', which helpfully anaesthetises your mouth until you can get to the dentist. (The slugs were particularly partial to this one last year... sadly it didn't numb their voracious mouthparts for good.)

The garden is divided into a series of spaces, with an ornamental area at the front, bordered by a pergola awash with climbing roses. Wide borders are densely packed with an eclectic mix of young trees such as *Catalpa bignonioides* 'Aurea' (the golden bean tree) and *Cercis siliquastrum* (the Judas tree), both of which thrive among a tapestry of shrubs, perennials and grasses.

Janet is especially pleased with the bed next to the front door which contains dwarf conifers, and around two hundred heathers – all grown from tiny cuttings. In flower throughout winter and early spring, they're covered with clematis in summer.

The herb garden occupies an L-shape around the back and side of the house. This is sub-divided by trellis – engulfed in clematis and honeysuckle – into a series of miniature gardens each dominated by a particular herb type or habit. There are carpets of low-growing marjorams, oregano and thymes; taller rues and rosemaries; tiny pathways bordered with violas and chamomile; and a container garden of around 90 different types of potted mint. There's even a cool chamomile seat to sit on, planted with the creeping *Chamaemelum nobile* 'Treneague'.

The garden is almost totally organic, despite an ongoing problem with slugs. 'This is a fantastic piece of countryside for birds,' says Maurice. 'We get greater spotted woodpeckers and a lot of song thrushes, which are in decline nationally, so the last thing we want to do is start putting chemicals down.' Instead, each night they collect slugs by the bucket-load and water the plants with a biological control called nematodes.

Although running the nursery involves a lot of hard work (repotting the mints takes a month each year) the Elliotts relish their new lifestyle. 'We haven't got as much money but we're better off in every other way,' says Janet with conviction. 'I rarely get ill. I suppose in a way I'm my own aromatherapist, constantly smelling and absorbing the oils.' Maurice agrees, 'Building work was ruthless. It's just as fascinating to manage and market the plants Janet grows, as it was building a new office block, and it's a lot less stressful.'

Janet grows most herbs from seeds and cuttings

Above: Oil from *Nardostachys grandiflora* (spikenard) was used to annoint Jesus' feet at the Last Supper. It has also been used to make rejuvenating cosmetics and as a balm in Hindi Ayurvedic medicine

Enchanted wood...

... or prehistoric swamp? Fairhaven Garden has the atmosphere of both, and is at its finest in spring.

Dappled sunlight casts an air of mystery... The glistening foliage of dryopteris and a pink confection of candelabra primulas conspire to seduce your senses

Fairytale wood

Above: Planting in layers creates a natural, sweeping effect. Hostas, geraniums and candelabra primulas create a colourful scene in May. Right: After the bright yellow flowers of the skunk cabbage have faded, their impressively huge leaves give a jungly effect

George Debbage is head gardener at Fairhaven. He's expanded the range of plants that thrive in the grounds while maintaining its role as a haven for local wildlife. 'Everything is grown organically and nothing is wasted,' says George. 'Leaves are composted and even dredgings from the dykes are used to mulch the borders.'

In the stillness of the early morning, the woodland and waterways of Fairhaven Garden have the strangely compelling atmosphere of a prehistoric swamp. All the giants of the plant world are to be found here: *Gunnera manicata*, slowly unfurling its majestic leaves; *Lysichiton americanus* (American skunk cabbage) throwing out its acid-yellow spathes, followed by great clumps of dark green cabbage-like leaves; and the brilliant colours of thousands of candelabra primulas, lighting up the paths and lining the waterways of this magical garden.

Set on the Norfolk Broads, Fairhaven is a wooded garden centred around a series of dykes populated by ancient alder carrs (boggy areas that have silted up), and criss-crossed by bridged pathways which spill onto higher, drier, woodland walks through groves of beech and oak.

The idea for a garden here was conceived by Henry Broughton, later to become Lord Fairhaven, who bought the South Walsham estate in Norfolk in 1947. He found a wilderness of fallen trees, brambles and nettles, but inspired by his friend, Sir Eric Savill, creator of Windsor Great Park, he set to work to create a new kind of naturalistic Norfolk garden.

As the dykes were cleared, he introduced shade and water-loving plants: primulas, skunk cabbage, hostas, camellias and rhododendrons imported from the Himalayas. The garden was hacked out of the undergrowth by Henry with the help of a woodman, whose successor, George Debbage, is head gardener today. 'I came here for three months in 1963,' George remembers, 'just to see me over a bad patch.' He's still here nearly 40 years later...

Staying faithful to Lord Fairhaven's vision, George has

Jungly giants

The drumstick primula (*P denticulata*) is a cheerful sign that spring has arrived. In shades of pink, purple and white it forms satisfying clumps, with spherical heads of small flowers. Thriving in sun or shade, and in moist soil, it can be propagated by seed, division or root cuttings.

Camellias benefit from the overhead canopy of trees, not only to filter strong sunlight but to give protection from frosts which can damage their early flowers.

Where there's space for its 2m (6ft 6in) wide leaves, *Gunnera manicata* lends a prehistoric, swampy feel to the garden.

Right: Wild alders love moist soil. They grow quickly and are ideal for attracting wildlife.

Escapist paradise

developed the garden, expanding its range of plants and extending its spectacular display of candelabra primulas. The original plantings were restricted to the corners of the dykes, designed to catch their reflections in the water. George found that if the weeds were kept at bay, the primulas seeded themselves further into the alder bogs. Taking this a step further, he started collecting the ripe seed and spreading it by hand along the edges of the new bridge walkways, with resounding success. The primulas have now colonised all the bridge paths and much of the wetland in between. 'They started the process,' says George, 'I just gave them a push. We're natural gardeners here, we assist nature.'

One of his main concerns is to encourage wildlife. To this end, the garden is kept totally organic, using only its own leaf soil as compost. 'We rake three miles of pathway every year,' smiles George wryly, 'so there's plenty of it.' He uses mainly oak and beech leaves as these rot down slowly to give the best compost. After storing it for two or three years, the leafmould is sifted and spread on the beds in autumn and early spring.

The leaves are raked just after Christmas ('If we did it before then, we know damn well we'd have to do it twice!'), and around this time George and his two gardeners also face the unenviable task of cleaning out all the dykes. They do this by walking through the icy water, dredging out the debris with cromes (long-handled forks with reflexed ends like curved rakes). 'If we do it early enough we can spread the waste straight on the beds and the plants will grow right through it.'

Then, in early spring, they fork over the borders. The edges of these flow seamlessly into the surrounding habitat and to the unpractised eye it's almost impossible to tell where nature leaves off and man takes over. Native ferns and *Petasites albus* (butter-burr) rub shoulders with the glaucous *Hosta sieboldiana elegans* and the graceful bamboo, *Pseudosasa japonica*. (The butter-burr made its name as nature's clingfilm – its broad leaves being used in days gone by to wrap up the butter to keep it fresh!)

Later in spring the garden is prepared to receive visitors by 'polishing the paths' (weeding, hedge-cutting, mowing and strimming). The strimmer is also used to nudge along the bluebells and primroses, flicking their ripe seedheads to spread them around.

It's surprising how, after more than 30 years, George's enthusiasm remains unflagging. 'Last season we made a new path, which we've called the Butterfly Path, along the edge of one of the dykes. We've got hemp agrimony, marsh thistle and purple loosestrife, and the butterflies love it.' He's also planning to extend the season of colour by increasing the range of cultivated plants in the garden. But definitely no herbaceous borders, he says, 'They wouldn't fit with the character of the place. We try to do everything carefully, keep it close to nature.'

The garden's a haven for wildlife – especially the butterfly path

During the winter George and his team manage the woodland by coppicing. Cutting mostly hazel as it has the straightest poles, they sell these to the Environment Agency (formerly the National Rivers Authority) which uses them for river defence on the Ouse. The coppiced hazel is formed into 'mattresses' of reed and hazel which are sunk into the river and weighted with rocks. These allow the water to flow through, trapping the silt to prevent erosion of the river bed.

Lord Fairhaven was a keen naturalist too, and created a bird sanctuary at the western end of the garden. More than 90 bird varieties have been recorded here, including snipe, water rail and the rare marsh harrier.

A pleasure boatman plies his trade from the old boathouse, but thanks to an ancient dispute between the landowner and villagers, the use of the Inner Broad is jealously guarded: no mooring, fishing or swimming is allowed. But the birds certainly aren't taking any notice: as well as mallards and moorhens, herons flap ponderously overhead, while tiny treecreepers spiral up willow trunks overhanging the water as cormorants bask in the sun to dry their wings. What better place to create a truly magical woodland garden?

Realise a dream...create

Fact: you don't need seven acres!

1 Provide shade. This is the first step in creating a woodland garden. You don't even need trees – the cool shade of a north-facing wall is better than a dense clump of large oak trees, and the soil will be more moist, too. At Fairhaven, trees are coppiced regularly to allow light to the plants beneath, otherwise choose small trees that cast dappled shade. Birches are ideal and their stems look lovely in winter. Plant Japanese maples between them to provide interest and colour.

2 Choose delicate plants such as the spring-flowering native *Anemone nemorosa* (wood anemone). This will spread into large carpets of foliage and pretty flowers, before the trees above are in full leaf.

3 Plant primroses. *Primula vulgaris* is the ideal choice for a bright, but tasteful display. These will light up your garden with spring colour and there's a huge selection to choose from. Don't dig up plants from the wild, buy young plants from garden centres. Either collect the seed or allow them to seed around. Primroses thrive in shade but cowslips *(P veris)* prefer a more open position.

4 Inject colour. If you crave more vibrancy in your garden, try polyanthus or candelabra primulas. With their tiers of flowers in every permutation of white, pink, magenta, yellow and orange, they create a dazzling display. Improve the soil with organic matter and make sure they never go short of water.

a woodland garden

3

4

GETTING STARTED

SOIL IMPROVEMENT

Woodland plants prefer soil that is rich in humus so dig in as much garden compost, well-rotted manure or mushroom compost as you can. After planting and in subsequent years, give a thick organic mulch to maintain moisture and add humus. Extra effort in preparation will mean you can grow a wider range of plants.

LUSCIOUS FOLIAGE

Because woodland gardens are at their peak in spring and it's difficult to find bright woodland flowers in summer, consider foliage plants to create interest. Among the best are:

● **Epimediums** – these clump-forming plants have pretty flowers in late spring but useful, weed-smothering foliage all summer.

● **Ferns** – both evergreen and deciduous ferns suit these shady conditions and provide a textural contrast to hostas.

● **Geraniums** – although some like full sun, many will tolerate shade and the more vigorous spreaders such as *G oxonianum, G sylvaticum* and *G phaeum* not only bloom for many weeks, their growth covers gaps left by plants that disappear underground for summer, such as wood anemones and celandines.

● **Hedera** – use variegated ivy as ground cover in tough places and as a background to spring bulbs.

● **Hostas** – in addition to their bold and beautiful leaves the spikes of pale flowers are a welcome bonus in summer. Avoid the large *H sieboldiana* types with corrugated leaves as these collect dirty drips from trees above.

● **Pulmonarias** – the attractive, spotted and blotched leaves look good long after the pink, blue or white flowers are forgotten.

● ALSO TRY: a few evergreen, structural shrubs such as sarcococca, viburnum and box. If your soil is acid, choose rhododendrons and camellias for their flowers and structure.

BULBOUS BEAUTIES

Many spring bulbs grow naturally in woodland and their early flowers are always welcome. Plant snowdrops and winter aconites, in the green – they'll get going more quickly than dried bulbs.

Woodland

fantasia

Bluebells are the essence of spring and anyone can enjoy them by taking inspiration from this fabulous garden.

The prime glory of Sally Owles' garden near North Walsham, in Norfolk, has got to be the bluebells. In May, sheets of them carpet the understorey of the woodland surrounding Sally's house, interspersed with young fern croziers unfurling like Catherine wheels in slow motion.

Sally's bluebells are native English ones, *Hyacinthoides non-scripta,* a species which is an integral part of our spring landscape. It has been known variously – and poetically – through the ages as wild hyacinth, witches' thimble, culverkeys, cuckoo's boots, ring o'bells and sapphire queen. Early botany books commented that bluebells were too well-known to require any description, although Gerard the herbalist (c 1597) commented on the strong, sweet smell

SALLY'S GARDEN

Where is the garden?
North Walsham, Norfolk

Garden history: Forty years ago, it was a commercial sycamore wood

Soil type: Sand covered by a thick layer of leafmould

Plants that thrive: Bluebells, camellias, rhododendrons, hellebores, primroses

Notable wildlife visitors: Badgers and bats

Any wildlife pests? Squirrels and deer

Bluebell tip: Sally plants bulbs 15cm (6in) deep to stop the squirrels eating them

Rhododendrons flourish in the light shade
and leafy soil

THE BLUEBELL FILE

Botanical Names: *Hyacinthoides non-scripta*, (formerly *Scilla non-scripta*, *Endymion non-scriptus*)

Flowering time: Late April or May, depending on area

Plant height: 20-45cm (8-18in)

When to plant: Sept-Oct

How to plant: In humus-rich but well-draining soil, in partial shade

How to propagate: Lift clumps and divide them as they die down. Collect and scatter seed

Scent: Has been likened to honey, spices or cinnamon

Notes: The English bluebell is now protected under the Wildlife and Countryside Act, so be sure to check, when you buy your bulbs, that they come from certified cultivated stock.

Hellebores, rhododendrons and Japanese anemones thrive under the woodland canopy

The fronds of ferns make the perfect partner
for bluebells

PHOTOGRAPHY: ANNE GREEN-ARMYTAGE

of the flowers.

Bluebells have been put to many uses over the centuries: bulbs were dried and powdered and used as a starch-substitute, both in cooking and for stiffening Elizabethan ruffs. The sticky secretion from the stalks was used as glue, in book-making and for sticking feathers to arrow shafts. The plant was also used medicinally as a cure for leprosy and, according to Tennyson, as an antidote to snake bites. We now know that all parts of the plant are poisonous, so presumably these two remedies were not particularly effective!

Bluebells love the damp but well-drained conditions in Sally's garden, which lies on a pocket of sand enriched by a thick layer of leafmould from the trees.

Sally and her father moved here in 1956 and at the time the land surrounding the house was a sycamore plantation. The timber was sold to a local broom manufacturer for handles and brush backs. Superseded by plastic, the wood was no longer needed and Sally decided to manage the grounds for pleasure rather than profit. She has gradually thinned out the trees, and wages an annual battle against sycamore seedlings. 'They come up like cress, so we have to spray them off,' she says dryly. 'I'd like to get rid of a lot of sycamores, particularly near the house, and put in trees that don't leave sticky sap all over everything!

'I love birches. With a birch tree you've something to look at all year: foliage in spring and summer, and the trunk and tracery of the branches during winter.'

This thinning out, coupled with the removal of vast numbers of brambles and briars, has allowed the bluebells to emerge. The leafmould has created a layer of humus-rich soil that forms the ideal habitat for woodland plants such as hellebores (*left*). It also means that many bulbs sit much deeper in the soil than conventional wisdom would suggest. 'I was quite surprised that some of them are nine inches, even a foot deep,' she says. 'The leafmould has built up on top of them over the years. If I was planting now I'd put them in about six inches deep, so they didn't get scratched up by the squirrels.'

Although grey squirrels are not Sally's favourite garden inhabitants, encouraging wildlife is a passion. Some areas she leaves deliberately uncultivated. 'You must allow nature some leeway,' she says firmly. 'You shouldn't manicure it. A tidy garden offers little shelter for animal and bird life.

Rhododendron luteum has flowers that smell of honeysuckle. After flowering, the foliage is bright and fresh, turning to gold in autumn

Erythronium dens–canis (dog's tooth violet) lifts its flowers above the marbled foliage as they unfurl

'A friend saw a badger last summer, lumbering up the drive at around 8.30pm at night, and at the moment we've got a very cross-looking bat roosting in one corner of the garden. It has the most peculiar screwed-up face!

'I curse the deer and the muntjac, however, when they nip off all my flower buds. The plants do recover, and flower later than usual. You can't beat a moving landscape.'

Other plants that fit into the woodland environment include rhododendrons (*inset*), Japanese maples and camellias. Sally is very particular with her planting. She has been known to buy a plant, put it in the ground, only to dig it up again and give it to a friend because it doesn't fit in her garden!

Sally also digs out a few of her bluebells now and again, for friends, but is careful not to deplete her stock. You don't need a whole woodland to enjoy them – a damp but well-drained spot in the dappled shade of a deciduous tree or large shrub will give them all the light they need to bloom in spring and have a shady rest in summer. 'Watch where they are,' says Sally, 'and that's where they'll grow.'

Primroses thrive at the edge of woodland clearings

Young fern croziers unfurl like Catherine wheels in slow motion

ABOUT TERRY'S GARDEN...

Where is the garden? Worcestershire

How big is it? About half an acre

What's the soil type? The worst – cold, heavy, hard-to-dig clay...

Which direction does it face? The worst (again!) – north-east

Who do you share the garden with? Squirrels, rabbits, moorhens (which actually climb the trees and eat my apples!) pheasants, foxes, badgers and grass snakes. They all eat each other...

Best gardening advice? Have patience!

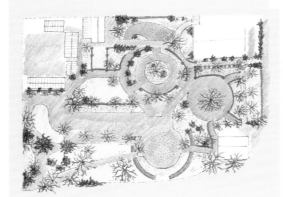

PHOTOGRAPHY: BOB ATKINS

The dazzling gold daffodil, 'Jetfire'...

..delicate white Anemone nemorosa...

the blue stars of chionodoxa...

and the velvety petals of polyanthus Gold–laced Group

Alive with spring colour

Very few gardeners are brave enough to invite the public into their garden in March. But when most of us are struggling to bring our gardens back to life, Terry Dagley's half-acre garden in Droitwich is already bursting with flowers. How does he get the garden up and running so early?

'The colour never really stops!' he says.

'The cyclamen start coming through in late summer, followed by the autumn species lilac crocus and pink colchicums. The first snowdrops are up by Christmas...'

Obviously, bulbs play a major role in the main spring display, set against a backdrop of evergreen trees and shrubs. After the snowdrops, crocus, starry blue scillas and chionodoxas, come hordes of

Terry's colour palette ranges the whole spectrum in spring

Pack out early displays with primulas and daffodils, available to buy ready–grown from garden centres. Pheasant optional...

Start spring early and share the planting brilliance of Terry Dagley's easy-care Worcestershire garden

white and yellow daffodils including frilly yellow 'Rip van Winkle', blue hyacinths and dwarf anemones, bluebells and myriad velvety primulas in sumptuous shades of maroon and gold.

'I only start mowing the lawn in June after the alliums have flowered,' explains Terry. 'Then in August we get the first cyclamen, so we stop mowing again. We've got one area measuring 20x30ft which is

completely full of naturalised pink and white cyclamen, and people are amazed when I tell them I didn't plant any of them! Their marbled foliage makes a very effective carpet of ground cover, too.'

This is a garden where colour reigns all year round. In Terry's opinion, 'bare soil is a waste of space, so for every bit of garden there are three plants - one visible, one about to flower and another poised to take

its place.'

With this heavy level of planting, Terry has a no-dig philosophy. So, instead of laying all his bulbs to waste with an annual dig-over, he simply hand forks very carefully to remove any weeds and only uses a spade or garden fork to remove the occasional unwanted shrub or tree.

One of the joys of a no-dig garden (apart from the obvious one) is that plants are left alone to produce seedlings. Nothing is deadheaded, the seed heads are left intact

'This is a garden where colour reigns all year round. Bare soil is a waste of space, so in every corner there's a succession of planting'

Above and right: Blue pulmonaria and pink primula 'Bon Accord Cerise' are great for a woodland-style garden in partial shade

to feed birds and mice, and inevitably when the plants self-seed they hybridise in the process, leading to some new and interesting plants. 'I let them fight it out and the most vigorous and strong survive,' says Terry. 'It's a system that soon sorts the wimps from the strong-growers!'

His primulas are a good example: 10 years ago, Terry bought five packets of old-fashioned seed from Barnhaven. One was Jack in the Green (with each flower surrounded by a ruff of green leaflets) another was Gold-laced (which looks more like an auricula with its neatly crimped gold edges and rich maroon flowers). Over the years, left to their own devices, these old-fashioned varieties have produced a diverse mix of new hybrids – a constant source of pleasant spring surprises.

Hellebores, pulmonarias and cyclamen are allowed to battle it out in just the same way, producing strong, healthy plants by natural selection. But no matter how vigorous these beauties are, it's hard to see them as 'thugs' as Terry calls them.

Of course, there have been a few vigorous bullies he wishes he'd never planted: stripy gardener's garters grass (*Phalaris arundinacea picta*, which has colonised the pond) and even the rampant lily of the valley. Yet these are thankfully still in the minority and there's an amazing range of choice shrubs, perennials and tender plants growing here too, the least hardy protected during winter with mounds of ash.

With his survival-of-the-fittest attitude it comes as no surprise that Terry prefers to garden along organic principles too. 'I do use pesticide on severe weeds, but I'm about 80 per cent organic.' As a result, his garden is full of wildlife come springtime – not least the nosy pheasant which posed for our photographers and will now take peanuts from Terry's fingertips. 'We've got squirrels, rabbits, foxes, badgers and grass snakes too. Unfortunately the latter two have eaten the hedgehogs, frogs and newts.' It's obviously a case of 'Survival of the Hungriest' where they're concerned...

IDEAS TO PINCH

ADD A LITTLE SPICE... with a giant spice jar. This one was made by Terry at pottery class (he used to teach the subject) but shop-bought ones can look just as charming once they've weathered.

CONJURE UP A LITTLE MYSTERY...
This unusual piece of sculpture is made from a couple of ancient quernstones, once used for grinding corn. Large shards of old stone are perfect for that 'ancient-druid' look, just plant a few medicinal herbs around the bottom!

ADD A SUNDIAL
This handsome time piece was made by Terry himself. To fire your own frost-proof clay pieces for the garden, sign up for pottery at your local nightschool

USE TREE STUMPS FOR SCULPTURE
Gnarled old tree stumps are perfect for adding natural shape and texture in your borders.

RECYCLE THOSE OLD WELLIES! Stuck for places to plant spring bulbs? Pop them in a pair of old green wellies, but don't forget to add drainage holes in the soles!

The colour garden

Discover how Diana Hemmings creates an explosion of summer colour using bedding mixed with perennials and shrubs.

DIANA'S GARDEN

Where is the garden?
Bristol

How big is it? It's short and wide – roughly 18x13.5m (60x45ft)

What's the soil type?
Loamy/clay – was rocky playing fields

Which direction does it face? South-west

Shares garden with:
Husband Sam and Ben the golden retriever

This pink and mauve confection comprises Surfinia petunias and fuchsias in a hanging basket, with clematis 'Jackmanii' and lavatera on the trellis behind. Clematis 'Princess Diana' climbs over an obelisk

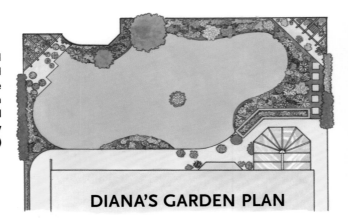

Diana's colourful borders surround an immaculate lawn, with pergola (top left) and conservatory (bottom right)

DIANA'S GARDEN PLAN

Borders brim with orange dahlias, orange and red snapdragons and pink *Malva moschata* ...

... fluffy ageratum, silver senecios, blue salvias, white lobelia and busy Lizzies

Colour-themed containers soften the bold outline of the patio

When Diana and Sam Hemmings moved to their new home in the smart Bristol suburbs four years ago, they had to start the garden from scratch. 'The soil was very hard, compacted clay, full of bindweed and rocks,' Diana explains. 'It was very windy, too, so many plants just got flattened.'

New gardens like this can take ages to establish. Often the most practical, short term solution is to go for colour – and lots of it! – by packing in plenty of annuals for instant impact, while waiting for perennials and shrubs to grow.

'Creating a new garden doesn't mean you have to ask *Ground Force*,' says Diana. 'Some people get landscapers in for six to eight weeks – costing a small fortune in the process. But all it really takes is some imagination, plus a bit of trial and error.'

'I love annuals for their colour. They're great for instant impact and filling in all the gaps. My favourites are the old-fashioned, scented sweet peas, which I grow from seed in the conservatory.' Other treasures grown from seed include ageratum, French and African marigolds, alyssum and morning glory – all planted out at the end of May.

Diana uses bedding all over the garden – intermingled with perennials such as clematis, dahlias, lilies and hollyhocks for an informal look. 'I originally set out to create a cottage garden feel. But every year I change

things around and move plants – the garden keeps evolving. The aim is, in the long term, to have something coming into flower all the time – at least until late September. In spring, as the daffodils, wallflowers, tulips and forget-me-nots fade they'll be followed by delphiniums, phlox and lupins, then dahlias and annuals take over in summer.'

Apart from offering a dazzling array of colours, annuals are useful problem-solvers, too. For instance, in the shady lee of a leylandii hedge at the bottom of the garden, Diana has planted a row of busy Lizzies to brighten the gloom where

Annuals are useful problem solvers – they fill gaps and add instant colour. Here snapdragons and pansies in citrus shades, velvety petunias and pink mallows grow under camellias

little else will grow. 'This year I'm trying nicotiana for a bit of height, and pansies, too,' she adds. And, along the top of a low wall around the conservatory she's planted a line of cheerful red pelargoniums and purple Surfinia petunias. 'Few other plants would manage in this exposed spot in such shallow soil.'

Colour-themed containers and hanging baskets help soften the bold outlines of Diana's new patio. 'I've got fuchsias, petunias, pelargoniums, blue ageratum and mini French marigolds in my containers. I try to create different colour schemes with them every year.

'I've also got some little flowerpots filled with nigella (love-in-a-mist) and eschscholzia grown from seed – they're ideal for popping into the ground whenever fresh gaps appear.' Not only will such gems nestle happily among perennials such as cordyline 'Torbay Dazzler', they'll also hide the untidy ankles of shrubs such as lavateras and roses – especially as they only have shallow roots and don't compete for soil nutrients or water.

Containers and baskets positively drip with Million Bells petunias, fuchsias and lobelia, helping to soften the harsh outline of new paving and brickwork

Ageratum, fuchsia and red petunias will flower until the first frosts of autumn

All around the garden Diana has used her colourful plants to add height, too, introducing hanging baskets at eye level filled with Million Bells petunias, fuchsias and lobelia, set off by trailing ivy. Then, to hide the new fences, Diana has spent the last two or three years training up a mix of honeysuckle, purple and white solanum, grape vines, clematis, climbing hydrangeas and roses. 'On one fence I've got the rose 'New Dawn' which has pale pink buds opening to white, while pinky-apricot 'Compassion' grows on the side of the house and 'Golden Showers' climbs up some trellis screening around the path – they're all trustworthy climbers which flower from the end of June into September – sometimes longer if I keep deadheading them.'

Festooned on all sides by such a glorious mix of flowers and foliage, it's hard to imagine what Diana's garden looked like four years ago. The corners are already looking established – one of them is damp and shady, with a small Japanese-style pebble water feature surrounded by lush green ferns, potted conifers and hostas, plus a couple of acers – one green, one copper – in containers.

With so many plants to care for, watering, weeding and deadheading could become quite a task by midsummer. 'I spend about six or seven hours pottering in the garden every week. It's not a chore though – I enjoy it! Fortunately the lawn is Sam's preserve and he mows it about twice a week in summer. Originally it had a lot of moss, but we used lawn sand and the odd bit of weedkiller and now it's looking very green and healthy. We're slowly making the borders bigger though, to make more space for plants...'

PLANNING YEAR-ROUND COLOUR

Keep the colour coming all year round.

Early spring

hellebores

Late spring/early summer

peonies

'Choose a colour scheme and stick to it. Magenta and scarlet will work diluted with green'

IDEAS TO STEAL

TURN LOW WALLS into a planting opportunity. Here a mix of colourful pelargoniums creates a sunny mood along a wall around Diana's conservatory – with spiky cordyline 'Torbay Dazzler' behind. They thrive in this dry, sunny spot, producing a mass of flowers. In richer soil they're inclined to produce leaves at the expense of blooms.

DISGUISE FENCES with tall pink hollyhocks and yellow dahlias, plus a selection of colourful climbers such as honeysuckle and roses. Here Diana has used vines for their shapely leaves, a hanging basket in the corner filled with petunias and massed annuals at the front.

LIVEN UP A SHADY HEDGE with a colourful fringe of busy Lizzies at its feet. They'll thrive in shade provided they don't go short of water. Diana has added a mulch of organic compost to retain moisture.

Midsummer

dahlias

Late summer/early autumn

Michaelmas daisies

Late autumn/winter

winter pansies

Frame wintry garden paths with neatly trimmed evergreens – shapely spheres of clipped euonymus 'Emerald 'n' Gold' and an arbour covered in swags of ivy

Create winter interest

Discover how to make your garden a magical winter oasis. Lyn and Peter Prior have mastered the art!

When most of us are battling against fallen leaves, tatty foliage and dreary bare patches in our borders, Lyn and Peter Prior have organised their garden, at The Little Cottage in Lymington, Hampshire, for a minimum of winter work and maximum impact. It's hard to believe their garden was once little more than lawn and crazy paving, but now it's jam-packed with beautiful plants for year-round colour and interest, with a pervading sense of style and structure – even in the depths of winter! We asked them how they did it...

First, study your site. Find out where the sunny and shady areas are, and what kind of soil you're gardening on. When Peter and Lyn bought The Little Cottage they soon discovered they were dealing with light, sandy, slightly acid

LYN AND PETER'S GARDEN

Soil type: Light and sandy

Faces: South

Time spent gardening: Every spare moment. It's where we want to be!

How long have you been here? 16 years

Are you organic? No

Shares garden with: Ophelia, our doddery Persian, and badgers

Top tip: Be prepared to spend money on good plants. They're worth it in the long run

77

'A winter garden doesn't have to be entirely green!'

soil. This is good news for winter gardening as the soil never gets too heavy or waterlogged, and also allows them to grow acid-loving evergreen plants such as heathers, some azaleas, rhododendrons and camellias. In hot summer weather, however, it means that all the plants need regular watering.

Next, create 'rooms'. This helps you to break down an unkempt winter garden into manageable chunks, where you can experiment with different seasonal planting groups and colour schemes. 'We both love structure,' says Lyn, 'and so subdivided the garden into five areas screened by high hedges.' Evergreen hedging and colourful trellis can also provide sheltered planting pockets, each with its own microclimate, allowing you to protect less hardy plants from winter frosts.

Once they'd established their framework of rooms, Lyn and Peter tackled one area at a time, making straight paths and geometric beds in circles, rectangles and squares. This formal layout helps create an orderly, neat impression – even when some of the late summer perennials are looking tired and straggly...

'At least I don't have to mow a lawn,' adds Peter. 'There isn't one! It's all intensively gardened.' Fill every square inch of soil with ground cover plants (such as ajuga, lamium, nepeta, heathers, conifers, hardy geraniums) that flower at different times of year. This will ring the seasonal changes and keep weeds at bay.

Introduce winter shapes. Lyn and Peter have used a wide variety of evergreen shrubs – hollies, ivies, yew, box, ceanothus, conifers and euonymus – many of them carefully trained and clipped into attractive forms.

For instance, their variegated 'Golden King' hollies have been cut into green and gold lollipops, ivy has been trained over the framework of a sheltered arbour, rich green cubes of box (*Buxus sempervirens* 'Suffruiticosa') line the paths while their 'Emerald 'n' Gold' euonymus has been trained into standards that resemble an avenue of evergreen miniature trees, and the bay has been clipped into pyramids.

Four topiarised cypress are planted where the two main paths cross, 'to create a feeling of formality,' explains Lyn. The flower beds are edged with ivy, while a woolly-leaved *Stachys byzantina* adds a gentle silvery note, with velvet leaves that help soften the scheme and look great covered in a delicate tracing of frost.

Spin the colour wheel. Finding a colour scheme is a great way of creating distinctive effects in your winter garden – it needn't be entirely green! The Priors' variegated euonymus standards take on a pink tinge in winter, the holly varies from dark purple-flushed bottle green to yellow,

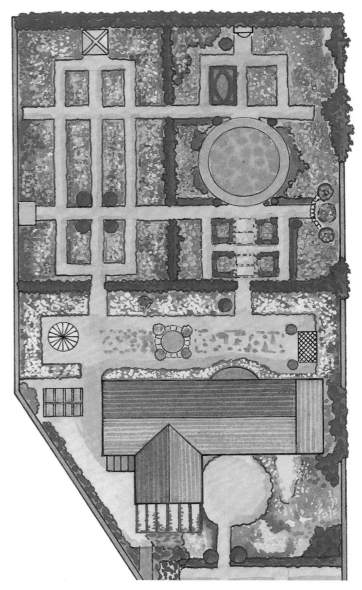

The Prior's garden measures 55 by 85 feet, faces south and has light sandy soil

while the ivies span silvery whites to butter yellow and purple.

Golden-leaved shade-lovers such as *Philadelphus coronarius* 'Aureus', *Physocarpus opulifolius* 'Dart's Gold' and *Choisya ternata* 'Sundance' are planted under a screen of ivy-covered trellis, while elsewhere, in the sea-green, mauve and silver area (which Lynn calls The Dell Garden), the evergreen foliage is a mixture of subtle blue-green and silver, with an arc of blue conifers - *Chamaecyparis lawsoniana* 'Pembury Blue' - as a backdrop for a curved garden seat.

Lyn has a discerning eye for colour which also guides her summer

THREE WAYS WITH GARDEN SEATS...

Make the most of a Gothic wrought iron chair by placing it under a trellis arch, against a painted wooden fence or panel

Turn your garden seat into a pretty focal point, leading the eye to it with a path and framing it with an ivy archway

For a blue finish, try Seagrass from Cuprinol (tel 01753 550555) or Shed Blue from Farrow & Ball (tel 01202 876141)

planting. In particular, she likes to combine different plants in the same colour range. 'I like to contrast form and shape. Imagine the spike of *Verbascum chaixii* 'Gainsborough' against the blob of a single rose, close to the trumpet shape of a lily with the fanned petals of a daisy – all in pale yellow.'

In her 'copper area' of the garden, where the summer flowers are pale peach and apricot, winter warmth and depth come from the bronze leaves of heuchera 'Palace Purple', dark-leaved berberis, coppery phormiums and cordylines providing looser structural shapes in winter that contrast well with the formal lines of the clipped evergreens.

Use arbours, statues and trellis for structure.
In the very depths of winter, when there's precious little in flower and deciduous plants have shed their leaves, make the most of your slumbering garden by incorporating attractive wooden, stone and metal structures. Lyn and Peter have introduced sheltered seats and wooden benches at strategic points all round the garden – not only as places to sit, but also as a focal point in their own right.

Above: Another clever idea – a multi-coloured glass teardrop windchime

Left: Classic lollipops of variegated euonymus help punctuate the winter planting

PHOTOGRAPHY: BOB ATKINS

Through this wrought iron gate, shaped like a spider's web, lies Danae's wild garden

Add Eastern tranquillity with a buddha

A garden for all seasons

Danae Johnston refuses to let her garden fade away during winter, demanding that it perform all year round

DANAE'S GARDEN

The garden: Seal Point, Luton

Soil type: Chalky

Position: North-west facing and on a slope

Garden size: Half an acre

Shares garden with: Ghyll and Tom the two black poodles

Top tip: Whenever I get a delivery of gravel from builders' merchants I use the canvas sacks to compost leaves

V isit Seal Point any day of the week, in any weather, and the odds are you'll find Danae Johnston in her garden. If she's not pruning, she's planting; if she's not planting, she's propagating in the greenhouse.

For this is an all-year garden grown mainly from seeds and cuttings. Not for Danae the bleak outlook of dead foliage and gappy borders once autumn comes along. She's fashioned a garden on a shoestring, full of choice shrubs and unusual trees which provide a skeleton she can flesh out with early-flowering bulbs, herbaceous plants and grasses as the seasons progress.

Not surprisingly, Danae is a firm believer in the value of having an overall plan. 'When we moved here 32 years ago, I laid out the plan on paper first. And although I haven't stuck to it exactly, it has stopped me muddling along.'

Hellebores are dusky winter beauties that will light up a January garden.

The burnished hues of autumn are well-represented with the crimson flowers of sedums adding vibrant splashes of colour beneath the golden-brown stems of grasses

Flaming autumn tints add a fiery glow

Right: Overhead plan

1. wild garden – bulbs
2. trees and shrubs
3. lawn
4. balcony and stairs
5. ponds
6. house
7. ornamental garden
8. herbaceous borders
9. curved border
10. bonsai
11. veg garden
12. cordons and soft fruit
13. greenhouse
14. shed
15. compost

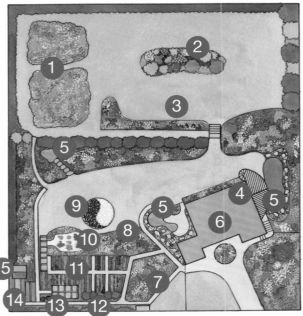

Miaow! Danae shows her skill at topiary with this carved box sculpture

GREAT PLANTS THAT GIVE STRUCTURE IN WINTER

1. Tall, slender conifers such as *Cupressus sempervirens* 'Stricta'
2. Clipped evergreen box
3. Upright cornus stems – choose between red, black or yellow
4. The leaves of *Helleborus argutifolius*
5. Large palmate leaves of *Fatsia japonica*
6. Marbled leaves of *Arum italicum* 'Pictum'
7. Globe-shaped habit of hebes such as *H cupressoides* 'Boughton Dome'
8. Spiky leaves of variegated yuccas
9. Erect grasses – *Stipa gigantea*
10. Seedheads of *Clematis tangutica*

One of Danae's first tasks was to plan the garden's structure - choosing trees and shrubs that will offer height, shape and form come winter time. Foliage plays a key role in this, but rather than choose specific plants, Danae looks for particular qualities instead - such as large, bold leaves. (Hence her choice of *Fatsia japonica*, with its enormous leaves and sculptural winter presence.) 'I design my borders by planting a good range of foliage plants, then intersperse them with plants that perform for a short time, so that there's something different happening every month.'

Once the garden's structure is established it's time to flesh out the skeleton with colours and textures. For winter, Danae has plumped mainly for restful bolts of green – holly, yew, skimmia and aucuba – rather than a melée of seasonal bedding. As a result, the garden has a vaguely oriental feel, elegant and subtle, stripped down to its essential elements.

Danae adores unusual trees too – for their fascinating bark textures in winter. Her favourites include *Prunus serrula* with its satin bark, *Acer griseum* (the paperbark maple), and a weeping cedar, *Cedrus atlantica* 'Glauca Pendula'. There's also a spectacular maple, the acer 'Silver Cardinal'. 'It has brilliant red bark on the new growth, and peels wonderfully when it gets older, plus the young foliage is pink and slightly variegated. It's a lovely all-year round plant, but is quite fast growing, so it needs a lot of space,' says Danae.

Birches also grow very well at Seal Point – their sunlit silvery trunks glowing starkly against the green.

Even in the very depths of winter, Danae's water features lend the soothing sound of movement to her garden. There are two pools close to the house so they can be enjoyed from indoors when it's too cold to go out. At the foot of the largest sits a stone dragon (made by Danae, hogging the kilns at evening class) backed with bamboo, down to which falls a curtain of melodically cascading water. This is Danae's favourite part of the garden, particularly when the 'sun comes round at 3pm on a summer's afternoon and lights up the waterfall'.

Danae says she'd rather be in her garden than anywhere else on earth and it's easy to understand why. Her garden has been created with love and timeless patience – quite the most satisfying way to create your ideal garden.

Make your

If you want to create your own unique ornaments, pots and sculptures, why not enrol on a pottery course with your local education authority? They're cheap and you'll soon be producing masterpieces to take home

You can buy gargoyles from garden centres, DIY stores and flower shows (these have the best selection)

own garden ornaments

Fancy a dragon in your garden? We can't promise you one like this, but you can order a terracotta dragon to stick on the end of a cane

Danae has sculpted this beautiful goose. If you don't have time to do this, buy a painted aluminium cut-out

Danae made this mystical-looking cat out of clay at home using a kiln at a local school. She started sculpting at a pottery class run by the local authority and this is an excellent way to make inexpensive sculptures

Keep a beady eye on all that's going on in your garden with an owl sculpture

Create your own sundial out of old pieces of slate. Danae bought her slate direct from a quarry in Wales when she was on holiday. It was cheap, as they were waste, and all she did was stick them together with mortar. Easy!

Henry Moore would approve of this modern moggie!

PHOTOGRAPHY: NICK JOHNSON

A narrow grass pathway crosses the garden making it feel a lot wider than it really is – a clever trick!

Perennial pleasure

TONY'S GARDEN

Size: One third of an acre, 50m long by 15m wide

Aspect: Runs from east to west

Soil type: Free-draining sand

A passion for plants, an artistic eye and a flair for design have all helped Tony Poulton create a garden of rooms, each with their own personality

Tony Poulton's training as an interior designer has had a great influence on the style and planting of his garden, giving him an eye for colour and the ability to see which plants work well together. He pays a lot of attention to texture, size and shape, as well as colour, especially when planting a new area. Large-leaved plants are used as punctuation throughout the garden, allowing your eye to pause briefly, before moving on.

Although the garden is quite long and narrow, Tony has used this to his advantage by splitting it into different areas. 'I was inspired by Hidcote to divide the garden, simply so that you don't see it all at once. That way, you'll find that it'll hold your interest.'

Near the house, a wide, south-facing border of blue and cream makes the most of the sun and creates an attractive focal point when sitting on the terrace. Directly opposite and providing a delicate visual contrast, are a mass of shade-loving plants – these all enjoy the soft northern light on this side of the garden. Sheltered by the gnarled branches of an old apple, hydrangeas, magnolias and a pittosporum provide a colourful and year-round backdrop against which dicentra, polygonatum, pulmonarias and hostas jostle for position. Informal and relaxed, with the traditional feel of a cottage garden, these borders have a joyful exuberance that lifts the spirits.

Silver-leaved plants such as lychnis abound in the white garden

This border is packed with plants including agapanthus, hemerocallis, salvias, nepeta, cynoglossum and viburnum

Macleaya cordata, Bowles' golden sedge and *Persicaria amplexicaulis* all compete for centre stage in this border

Tony keeps *Agave americana* 'Mediopicta' in a container so he can bring it in during winter as it's only hardy to 5°C

This frothy planting helps soften the harsh vertical lines of the garden's most prominent feature – an extremely tall privet hedge. 'It was very neglected when I moved in, I gave it plenty of attention', says Tony. It's now 2.4m high with a central archway leading to the borders beyond. Two containers frame the opening and are planted with *Pelargonium* 'Fascination', *Fuchsia* 'Flash', verbena and *Tropaeolum* 'Empress of India'. The silvery-grey foliage of *Plectranthus argentatus,* pyrethrum and *Helichrysum petiolare* are effective companions.

Beyond the hedge, and using its green, textured magnificence as a backdrop, is a large herbaceous border packed with flowers of lavender, purple and pink. A narrow green path stretches from left to right drawing you to a paved area with a pedestal at one end and a gazebo clothed with scented climbers at the other.

An old wooden bench positioned here provides the perfect place to sit and contemplate. Completely enclosed, it's a delightful inner sanctuary where you can collect your thoughts.

The grass pathway brings an abrupt change in direction and, like the hedge, helps break up the garden into smaller areas. Acting as a strong horizontal axis, it makes the garden feel wider and slows the pace. It's almost as if Tony is saying, 'Come, on, relax and enjoy this garden!'

A weathered stone pathway meanders from beneath the gazebo towards the white garden, via a small avenue of containerised box plants and rustic arbour. The sudden formality of this topiary sets off the unstructured planting in the beds, with white-flowered plants and silver-leaved perennials cascading over the gravel path and up against the rigid green trellis

The lily 'Pink Perfection' scents the air and adds colour

It's a delightful inner sanctuary where you can collect your thoughts

Create garden rooms

The arbour adds height and the box balls in containers add formal structure, creating another change in mood

behind. It's a charming spot with pale, calming colours and a weathered stone birdbath – an ideal centrepiece surrounded by *Epilobium angustifolium,* white rosebay willow-herb, *Rosa* 'Iceberg' and *Eryngium variifolium.* A rose border on the south side and a spring garden on the north, with hellebores and pulmonarias, complete the scene.

In contrast, the flaming red, orange and yellow blooms of the hot border beyond the gazebo create more vibrancy with the individual flowers jumping out like fiery sparks. Ornamental poppies add their transient beauty to this bed in May, while salvias peak in summer and dahlias later during autumn.

Tony grows many different varieties of annuals, all from seed, and these are sown direct into the soil at the end of April. Again, shade-loving plants make the most of the northern aspect against the other fence. The garden was once home to the National Plant Collection of lobelias and they're still one of Tony's favourite perennials because 'they give such a good show late in the season'. Slugs are a problem but he admits watering the plants with SlugClear which controls them.

The final and most productive area of the garden is hidden behind a border packed with a fascinating mix of bronze, salmon and brown flowers. An unusual choice but one that works well.

His greenhouse and coldframes are the site of much activity in spring, with many early starts and late finishes as he prepares the garden for its main summer display. He takes plenty of cuttings and enjoys sowing annuals each year.

'They're great for filling gaps and normally last a long time. The secret of success with cuttings is to use a very free-draining mixture with plenty of grit. You'll often find me working from sunrise to

Screening is essential to hide any less attractive areas, but few gardeners make full use of the potential, missing the chance to plant colourful climbers up the trellis

The lower lawn mirrors the upper lawn, adding symmetry to the garden. In a well-designed garden the scale of the planting and main features is important. Symmetry usually works well. The wide border at the end creates an almost visual fullstop to the garden and hides the working areas behind

sunset in spring. It takes a lot of work to keep the garden looking its best. Deadheading is essential.' The garden is home to a wide range of plants from all over the world and appeals to those gardeners who like a strong element of design. 'I hope this garden has a little something for everybody and that I've created a balance between the planting and the design.'

However, it's clearly a time-consuming hobby. 'Try anything labour-saving!', he

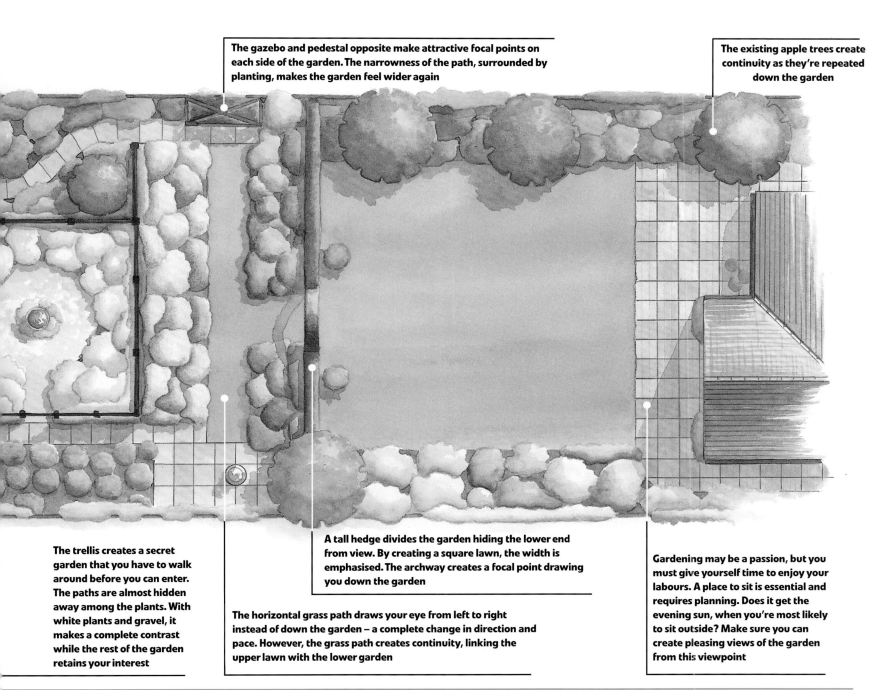

The gazebo and pedestal opposite make attractive focal points on each side of the garden. The narrowness of the path, surrounded by planting, makes the garden feel wider again

The existing apple trees create continuity as they're repeated down the garden

The trellis creates a secret garden that you have to walk around before you can enter. The paths are almost hidden away among the plants. With white plants and gravel, it makes a complete contrast while the rest of the garden retains your interest

A tall hedge divides the garden hiding the lower end from view. By creating a square lawn, the width is emphasised. The archway creates a focal point drawing you down the garden

Gardening may be a passion, but you must give yourself time to enjoy your labours. A place to sit is essential and requires planning. Does it get the evening sun, when you're most likely to sit outside? Make sure you can create pleasing views of the garden from this viewpoint

The horizontal grass path draws your eye from left to right instead of down the garden – a complete change in direction and pace. However, the grass path creates continuity, linking the upper lawn with the lower garden

advises. 'I grow a lot of perennials, which take a bit of maintaining. Perhaps shrubs would be better. But then, they need pruning...'. I think deep down, he loves his garden as it is and who can blame him?

'I hope that I've created a balance between the planting and the design'

Create a bigger impression

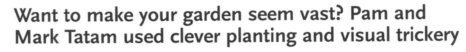

Want to make your garden seem vast? Pam and Mark Tatam used clever planting and visual trickery

Funny how a garden never seems quite big enough for all the gorgeous new plants you want to squeeze in! But Pam and Mark Tatam think they've found the answer – using a range of cunning visual tricks that make their Lincolnshire farm garden seem massive.

'People are always saying our garden seems bigger than it is,' says Pam. 'I put this down to the fact it's divided up into smaller areas so overall, it seems much larger.'

One of the first things they did was divide the garden into a series of self-contained areas, each with its own spectacular planting scheme to make the most of the space. There's a rose garden, a pond area with gravel garden and a sunken knot garden, all connected by meandering pathways and benches that encourage you to dawdle.

'We wanted a sunken garden to introduce a change of levels,' explains Pam's farmer husband Mark, who excavated the area in just one day using a mini digger. 'Different heights create an extra dimension in a small garden, so even if you can't make it physically bigger, at least you can vary the height of it, with steps and raised beds.'

MAKE A BIGGER IMPRESSION WITH...

PHOTOGRAPHS: BOB ATKINS

...giant orange dahlias such as 'David Howard' – you can't miss these flaming beauties with their dark bronze foliage!

...giant herbaceous borders à la Gertrude Jekyll and grassy paths which become narrower as they get further away to make the garden look longer. The bounding hound here, Islay, is actually a pocketsize shih-tzu

Struggling to find more planting space? Dig up the lawn and plant up a gravelly grotto like this instead. Here the profusion of flowers includes orange nasturtiums, red pelargoniums and yellow bidens. The strange black grassy plant at the front is *Ophiopogon planiscapus* 'Nigrescens'

This red-hot collection has salvia at the front, crocosmia behind, bronze heleniums and creamy yellow achillea. Perfect for a sunny spot

Another clever idea was to create two massive late summer herbaceous borders, each 4m deep. The grassy path between them narrows at the end, creating the impression that the borders are even longer than they actually are. 'Well stocked borders like these hide a multitude of sins,' confesses Pam. 'This is my favourite view of the garden. You can see it from my bedroom window where you're just far enough away to see all the colour and shapes, but not close enough to notice the weeds!'

In a small garden, plants really have to earn their keep across the seasons and the Tatums' stunning collection of trees and shrubs is the perfect example. In autumn the leaves of *Liquidambar styraciflua* (sweet gum), *Aronia melanocarpa* and *Cotinus* 'Grace' all flare up vivid orange and red before they fall. Come winter, plants with polished stems come into their own – *Prunus serrula* (Tibetan cherry) with its turned mahogany bark and *Eucalyptus pauciflora* (Australian snow gum) with its trunk striped red, white and blue like a tie-dyed Union Jack. *Sedum* 'Herbstfreude', and the evergreen grass *Stipa arundinacea* make a striking combination under the cotinus, which leafs up very late in spring. 'I've planted a 'Pompon de Paris' rose underneath it,' explains Pam. 'It flowers at the end of May and scrambles through the cotinus to bloom as its leaves unfold.'

In the rose garden, Pam's happy to wait all year for her favourites to bloom. 'They flower just the once but they're so sweetly scented... and I love the sense of anticipation I get while waiting for them to come out.' Their musky perfume fills the air during June as lines of rambling 'Princesse Louise' roses clamber over the top of an ironwork tunnel made by husband Mark.

The rose tunnel leads to a circular garden centred by a huge stone trough that's surrounded by *Lavandula intermedia* 'Hidcote Giant'. This in turn is ringed by a circle of lawn, encircled by a bank of catmint, Nepeta 'Six Hills Giant'. 'The bees and butterflies love this part of the garden,' says Pam. 'It just shows how effective bold drifts of lavender can be. I cut mine back twice a year with a hedge trimmer to stop it getting straggly – once in the autumn to take off the flower heads and again in spring to tidy it up.'

Bold circles of grass and gravel, mirrored by round islands of planting, can quickly banish the small-and-boxy look. 'Circles are easy to work around and just seem to fit,' agrees Mark. Perhaps they're magic circles? They've certainly worked wonders here.

CHOOSE EASY PLANTS THAT WILL EARN THEIR KEEP...

Pink sidalcea thrives in any soil in a sunny spot, and makes a great cut flower for a vase, too.

Purple agastache flowers June to October with aniseed scented leaves. Fragrant white petunias trail from the pot

The pretty purple stems of *Verbena bonariensis* appear from July to September and reach a statuesque 1.8m (6ft)

VISUAL ILLUSIONS TO TRY AT HOME

1 Create a meandering path through the garden so it takes you more time to explore it, with a comfy seat at the end.

2 Lead the eye up – using climbers, wall planters, steps and raised beds – to take emphasis away from limited ground space.

3 Use the old mirror trick. Make a wall or fence seem further away with a strategically-placed mirror – or mural.

4 Paint walls and fences a paler colour to make them seem further away.

5 Plant pale flowers at the end of a border to visually extend it.

"We made our garden look three times bigger..."

Paula Caiger and Dave Brown used clever design, water and soothing foliage plants to turn their claustrophobic city garden into a relaxing retreat with a more spacious, airy feel.

A built-in bench makes the most of a tight corner, with a pot of herbs as a centrepiece on the table containing ginger mint (*Mentha gracilis* 'Variegata'), sage and chives.

I f you've ever been stuck in a lift, you'll know how I felt when we moved here," laughs Paula Caiger, an art teacher from East London. "It was so claustrophobic – just a small lawn and two borders. You could see everything at once and all you could do was walk to the top of the garden and back again. I felt like a caged animal!"

Measuring 16 x 33ft (5x10m) Paula's garden might not be the smallest in the city, but she knew it was crying out for style, atmosphere and intrigue. Although Paula had been a competent gardener since childhood, she admits she was stumped when faced with this tiny plot. Her partner Dave – a quantity surveyor and creative handyman – had never gardened before, so one night they got together over a bottle of wine with a garden-designer friend, William, to devise a plan.

"William thought the best solution was to divide the space in two," explains Paula. "He had this idea of creating two separate sitting areas – a sun ray-shaped deck right outside the back door, and a raised, pentagon-shaped patio tucked away into the far left hand corner, both linked by a curvy slate path."

PHOTOGRAPHY: ANNE GREEN-ARMYTAGE

Soothing blue-and-green foliage creates a mood of calm in the smallest of urban spaces. Here a slate path creates a zig-zag to a raised patio, flanked by (on the left) frothy white *Campanula lactiflora* 'Loddon Anna' and spiky blue stems of veronica. On the right (in the foreground) is a pot of *Ligularia dentata* 'Desdemona', with the yellow flowers of santolina behind and pink *Geranium pratense* 'Spinners'.

We're Paula Caiger and Dave Brown. Paula is an art teacher and Dave is a quantity surveyor

How long have you been gardening? For 11 years but it only took four years to make the garden look as good as this

Where's the garden? Walthamstow, East London.

How big is it? 16 x 33ft (5x10m)

What's the soil like? Neutral loam

Which direction does it face? North, so the patio at the end gets the most sun

What's your favourite plant? Hostas and giant rhubarb – especially as its amazing leaves are unfurling in spring

Greatest success? The pond – it's only tiny but it's taken on a life of its own with all the frogs and toads it brings in, and the good they do in the garden

Most dismal failure? Clematis – we planted two to twine through the golden hop but both died from clematis wilt

What would you do differently? The decking planks were staggered to look like a sunburst but we had to saw off the ends as we kept tripping over them!

Wisteria sinensis winds luxuriously round the front door.

Pack the plants in nice and tight to keep the weeds down, says Paula. Here the blue patio door leads to a sun ray–shaped deck and pots containing hosta 'Zounds' and the rice paper plant (*Tetrapanax papyrifer*), bottom right.

William's design is clever on several counts: not only has it doubled the garden's potential by splitting the space in two, but by removing the square patio, lawn and straight path, he's made the garden seem less 'boxy'. The fact that the sitting areas are positioned in opposite corners of the garden helps too: the path forms an appealing zig-zag between them, literally side-stepping the problem of seeing all the garden at once from the back door. The whole thing works because the eye is tricked into believing the garden is much longer than it is, with the suntrap patio at the back hidden away behind plants. It's somewhere private to settle back in the sun and enjoy a reverse view of the garden.

They started work one spring weekend, with

There's always room for a stylish water feature... this one is made from stainless steel air conditioning ducts!

Dave taking charge of lifting turf, laying the planks for the deck and mixing cement for the concrete patio. Paula got stuck in too, and together they managed to build the lot in two weeks over the Easter holiday. Paula used the time to devise a unified colour scheme – soothing blues and greens, with terracotta highlights – which would ultimately dictate

not only the colour of the walls (painted in a contrasting orange), slate path and pots, but even the sea-blue tones of the gorgeous frothy leaves and flowers.

Eleven years on, you'd never know that the garden once looked so poky. Stepping out from the back door, you can't even guess where the garden ends – even though in

reality it comes to an abrupt full-stop just 10 yards away. Looking back at the house, what stands out are the blue French doors and flower-filled lead containers – guttering hoppers that Dave managed to salvage from a demolition site. The whole effect is calm and very tasteful – as perfect as a courtyard garden at Chelsea Flower Show, transferred lock,

The overhead view from the bedroom window reveals the clever use of a zig-zag layout, which means that, at ground level, you can't see the entire garden all at once. The giant stripy grass in the middle is *Miscanthus sinensis* 'Zebrinus'.

stock and barrel to Walthamstow.

Of course, as so many make-over TV shows have proved, paths, patios and pots alone do not a garden make! The fuzzy froth of evergreen rosemary and silver-leaved artemisia which jostle at the patio's edge, along with clouds of flowers and twining climbers lounging along the fence-tops, all serve to blur the boundaries and complete the illusion of having extra space. Paula's gone for a mix of sun and shade-lovers, all happy in her loamy London soil and selected for their wonderful blue and terracotta tones, inspired by one of Paula's favourite artists.

"Gustav Klimt – I love his paintings," she says. "When I was choosing the plants I had this image of his orchards and birches, and I've tried to get the same effect with blocks of coloured foliage. I'm always telling my art students to keep sketchbooks, so I practise what I preach by ripping out pictures of gardens and colours that grab me from newspapers and magazines."

Paula adores foliage, especially those show-stopping architectural plants with large, jungly leaves. Fortunately, you don't need many of these handsome big-leaved plants to create a feeling of largesse, breaking up the mass of smaller leaves

which could end up looking a little dull. Hosta 'Frances Williams', with its enormous green and blue leaves, has lived happily in a container for years; an ideal spot out of the way of slugs. Just to be doubly sure, Paula wraps the rim with slug-repelling copper tape.

Paula's love of foliage and her city location don't make for a good combination when it comes to slugs, which love the dank conditions. Here, there are endless daytime hideaways under cool pots and paving stones, with gourmet leaves at every turn. Instead of using pellets, Paula gardens organically, tempting in slug-eating wildlife, such

"I love slugs – I find them fascinating... I still can't kill them.

How the garden fits together

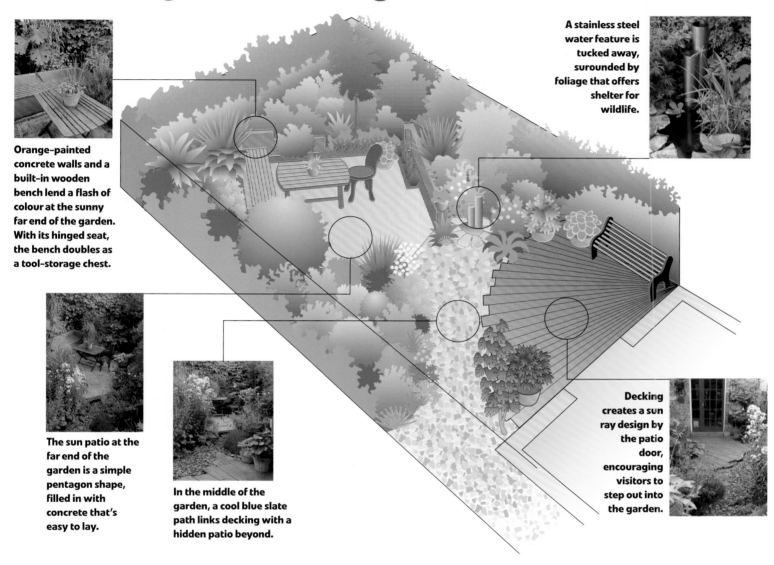

A stainless steel water feature is surounded by foliage that offers shelter for wildlife.

Orange-painted concrete walls and a built-in wooden bench lend a flash of colour at the sunny far end of the garden. With its hinged seat, the bench doubles as a tool-storage chest.

The sun patio at the far end of the garden is a simple pentagon shape, filled in with concrete that's easy to lay.

In the middle of the garden, a cool blue slate path links decking with a hidden patio beyond.

Decking creates a sun ray design by the patio door, encouraging visitors to step out into the garden.

as frogs and hedgehogs, with a pond. For Paula, the insect and animal life is at least as interesting as the plants and incredibly, even admits to having a soft spot for slugs!

"I love slugs, in fact all garden bugs – I find them fascinating. It was only when I started gardening that I realised what a pain they were. I still can't kill them though. I shouldn't say it, but I put them in the wheelie bin and forget about them..."

Given the lack of space here, and her penchant for rich, abundant planting, Paula has to take measures to keep the plants from taking over. Staking is essential to prop up taller species – especially where sun-loving plants are grown at the limits of their shade endurance and they start to get drawn. To keep things tidy, Paula has made her own stakes from wreaths of thin copper tubing, plunged into the ground behind the drooping stems. And this year, for the first time since they completed the garden four years ago,

I just put them in the wheelie bin and forget about them."

Paula will have to begin lifting and dividing her larger plants. "I'm going to put it off until this autumn though, so the garden still looks packed when we open it to the public through the National Gardens Scheme this summer. Last year, we had 200 visitors in a day. Thankfully not all at once!

"We had a hosta raffle in the street, so I could stall people outside if it got too crowded. It's a great way to meet new gardeners and if you don't like spending too much money on plants, you can get loads of cuttings and plant swaps. I'm always meeting people who are in the same position as I was 11 years ago, and I love showing them what's possible. At the end of the day, you just need to start somewhere and that should be by deciding what you like."

SPACE SAVING IDEAS

In a small garden where planting space is at a premium, make the most of your walls and fences by training plants to climb up wires or trellis, and placing trailing plants in wall containers to dangle down. Here, Paula has used a mix of ideas (clockwise from top left): trailing Lobelia is planted in a salvaged lead hopper and positioned on top of a wall for flowers dangling at eye level; grape vine Vitis vinifera clambers up the house wall on some rusty metal trellis – it turns yellow-gold in autumn; classic beauties *Jasminum officinale* and honeysuckle *Lonicera japonica* 'Halliana' create a dainty contrast of white flower forms against a side wall.

BLENDING BLUES WITH WARMER HUES

Blue leaves create an atmosphere of calm and restfulness – just the thing for gardens surrounded by bustling, built-up cityscapes. Yet blue plants on their own can look a little gloomy in a shady courtyard with high walls, and

Paula has found that by mixing her blue foliage plants with cheerful orange walls and exotic-looking succulents, it takes the cold edge off her planting scheme. Some of Paula's favourites are pictured below (left to right): *Macleaya*

cordata (the plume poppy) needs some sunshine and can be a bit of a thug if you don't watch out for runners and chop them off, H2m, S1m; *Sempervivum* 'Damask' is hard as nails as long it doesn't get too soggy, H and S 5-10cm; *Sedum* 'Autumn Joy' is another

toughie with plump succulent foliage and fresh rosy heads in August, H and S 40cm; *Sempervivum* 'King George', H and S 5-10cm; the ribbed leaves of *Hosta* 'Frances Williams' enjoy light shade and protection from slugs. H65cm, S1m.

Create a big impression...

Red geum 'Blazing Sunset' clashes wonderfully with geranium 'Pink Spice' under *Robinia pseudoacacia* 'Frisia' around a winding path

THEA'S GARDEN

Where is the garden?
Sutton, near Ely, Cambs

How long have you tended the garden?
Seven years

How big is it? 21x12m (70x40ft)

What's the soil type?
Dry and clay – on a slope

Which direction does it face? South

Want to make a small garden seem to go on forever? Thea Kybird has designed her sloping Cambridgeshire plot to pack in hundreds of plants and still maintain the illusion of space

Thea Kybird's south-facing garden seems to meander forever! It isn't vast – only 40 feet (12m) at its widest. But it winds up and around her Cambridgeshire bungalow, weaving from one plant-packed slope to the next, with broad, sweeping paths and deep, curvaceous borders.

Sutton
nr.
Ely

7. Lawn Lane

A broad grassy path helps organise the planting space and leads the eye through yellow coreopsis, deep pink diascia and pale pink *Geranium pratense* Summer Skies, towards a sizzling red alstroemeria

Thea Kybird deadheads the petunias in a hanging basket

'Curved borders, winding paths and stepping stones draw the eye and entice you to wander around'

The best way to create a sense of spaciousness like this is through the garden's structural layout. Even the tiniest plot can seem larger if you give it a framework that suits its size, shape and scale. Thea has done just that – dividing her garden into self-contained areas, then combining plants and permanent features to make the most of each separate space.

'As the garden is on a slope, one of the first things we did was level it in a couple of places, building a circular patio at the top of the garden with a sundial and shady arbour, and a square one for my container plant collections – hostas in the shade and alpines in the sun.' The latter grace old butler's sinks and homemade troughs covered with hypertufa (a mix of sand, cement and peat). 'Whenever I hear of someone throwing out an old sink I'm there like a magnet!' Thea laughs.

Next she and husband Dick tackled the pathways. 'I'm really into curved borders, winding paths and stepping stones – we've used them all round the garden linking one area to the next. They draw the eye and make you want to wander round and explore the next bit.' Thea's curving grassy path idea is an excellent way to create wider borders, without losing the lawn entirely.

To create plenty of planting variety – which always compensates for lack of space – Thea has subdivided her garden into a diverse range of habitats. A shady corner beside the kitchen is colonised by ferns and various ivies, while dappled shade from small trees allows for an exuberant mix of perennials and annuals. 'The dappled shade is essential,' says Thea, 'otherwise the sloping southern aspect would prove too much for most plants, even for my sun-loving penstemons!'

Another space-saving idea is to use trellis, obelisks and posts to create extra height. This has proved essential in Thea's garden as she's a confirmed clematis-addict. They're everywhere – intermingling with the roses, climbing up through shrubs and trees, scrambling over obelisks and weaving through ivy and golden hop.'I'm fascinated by them,' she explains. 'I love to see the flowers, and after them the seedheads when they catch the sunlight.'

Thea has around 65 different cultivars, and it's her ambition to enjoy a succession of clematis flowers throughout the year. And, with different varieties suitable for most conditions, she can plant them all around the garden – in sun and shade – although in open situations she finds it useful to grow each plant through a sturdier host, such as ivy and elaeagnus which are better able to withstand the wind.

Penstemon 'Evelyn'

With clematis springing up in every corner, Thea has also made sure she has a good variety of reliable evergreen shrubs to act as a year-round counterfoil – cotoneaster, pittosporum and laurel among them. These provide a solid backbone of neutral green, helping to make the seasonal flowers look all the more bright and dazzling.

Gardening on a slope means the soil is

Make your garden seem twice the size by reflecting it in a mirrored water feature, like Thea Kybird's

How's this for gorgeous ground cover? *Geranium pratense* 'Plenum Caeruleum'

White *Campanula persicifolia* 'Chettle Charm' and deep blue *C glomerata* 'Superba' jostle among chives and hostas, forming a colourful fringe around the patio

'I dedicate one whole day to housework, then spend six in the garden! I just love it.'

naturally very free-draining, and plants need a lot of watering to establish successfully. 'Even after wet winters I have to water-in any planting I do at the top of the garden,' says Thea, 'because once I've gone down about nine inches it's as dry as dust.' Nowadays she alleviates the problem by mulching with manure to retain moisture and condition the soil. But once a plant is well-established she lets it fend for itself: 'Watering a mature plant is a bad thing to do,' she maintains. 'You're bringing the roots up to the surface rather than letting them go down to find the moisture.'

Thea only truly regrets her slopes when she's pushing the mower around. 'I think the hill has lent something to the garden,' she says, 'although the structure has had

to be considered carefully, and I do have to support a lot of my plants against the wind. But I'm gradually learning. With perennials I use linked stakes and try to hide them so nobody can see them. And this year I've used scented petunias in most of my hanging baskets, rather than fuchsias, which tend to snap off in a gale.'

Thea's garden is most definitely not low-maintenance – she estimates she spends an average of four or five hours each day outside during summer, often longer. 'Some days I'll go out there at eight in the morning and come in at nine at night,' she laughs. 'I dedicate one whole day to housework, and then I can look forward to six days in my garden. I'm always out there, even in winter. I just love it.'

MAKE MORE SPACE IN YOUR GARDEN

1 First get rid of any space-hogging, overgrown trees and shrubs you don't like.

2 Organise the garden into distinct planting areas, using trellis, pergolas and bold, evergreen shrubs to make dividers.

MEET THE STARS OF THEA'S CLEMATIS COLLECTION...

'Proteus' prefers shelter but will do well in any sunny aspect. Double flowers appear in June followed by single, pale mauve ones in July. H 2.5m (8ft)

'Abundance' likes a sunny spot, flowering from July to October. Try growing it through a purple-leaved shrub shuch as cotinus. H 3m (10ft)

Clematis rehderiana flowers July to October with nodding cream bells, scented like cowslips. Grow it against a sunny wall or fence. H 6m (20ft)

Clematis cirrhosa balearica is a winter and early-spring flowering variety which prefers a sheltered corner. It's fragrant and evergreen. H 2.5m (8ft)

Clematis florida **'Plena'** flowers in early summer with a further flush in early autumn. It needs a sheltered position and protection from severe frost. H 2.5 (8ft)

'Prince Charles' teams well with roses as it flowers from June onwards. It'll flourish in most gardens, but as with all clematis, keep the roots cool. H 3m (10ft)

3 Link each planting area with winding paths in different patterns and textures – gravel, paving and lawn – for visual variety.

4 Turn your lawn into a broad grassy path to make the borders deeper and create more space for plants.

5 Use curves and circles – these help make narrow areas seem broader and encourage visitors to linger.

6 Create height with an obelisk (left). This will lead the eye upwards and take emphasis off the lack of space at ground level.

7 Use tall plants to mask fences and walls to reduce the 'hemmed in' feeling.

8 Use see-through trellis 'windows' and archways to give tantalising glimpses of the views beyond.

9 Create a dappled, shady area with a small tree to vary the habitats for planting and wildlife.

10 Use pale colours at the end of the garden – this creates the illusion of distance.

Pat's sculpture takes centre stage among colourful courtyard planting, with variegated pittosporum behind, white foxgloves, deep pink gladioli and yellow perennial poppies

The garden
gallery

Sculptor Pat Rae's tiny London courtyard is a restful haven filled with trees and plants in pots and a tranquil koi pool. It's the perfect place for displaying her works of art

Deep in the heart of South London, shut off by high walls from a haze of traffic fumes and incessant noise, Pat Rae's courtyard garden is a private oasis of clear air and quiet contemplation. It's the perfect place for a creative soul to let her imagination run free. Pat's a prolific artist and sculptor, and her walled garden reflects her love of colour, texture and form.

'All my work is organic,' she says. 'Everything I do is about nature and my relationship with it.'

Pat's garden and sculpture have evolved together over the 30-odd years she's been living here. When she first moved in, however, the site was a scene of dereliction and decay. 'It had been a distribution centre for a battery company,' she explains. 'There

ABOUT PAT'S GARDEN...

Where is the garden? South London

How big is it? Roughly 12x4.8m (40x16ft) at its widest

What's the soil type? Solid London clay, improved with home-made compost

Which direction does it face? The door looks west – it's a very shady garden

Best gardening advice? Know your soil

Shares garden with: Tigger the cat, frogs and fish.

PHOTOGRAPHY: ANNE GREEN-ARMYTAGE

Pots deter the family cat from eating the fish

PAT'S GARDEN PLAN

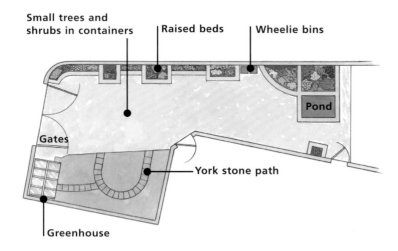

Small trees and shrubs in containers

Raised beds

Wheelie bins

Pond

Gates

York stone path

Greenhouse

Pat's koi pool enjoys a fringe of leafy container plants, including lemon verbena and *Acer palmatum dissectum*. The dark, etched paving creates a Japanese feel

were lots of old-fashioned batteries leaking everywhere and the adjoining stable block was full of oil. It hadn't been lived in for four years, there were holes in the roof and ceiling, no water and only one electric socket!'

THE L FROM HELL

After undertaking a large part of the renovation herself (including rewiring the entire house!) Pat turned her attention to the courtyard. This was an L-shaped stretch of concrete with virtually no soil, but little by little she built raised beds – initially over the concrete, but latterly, taking out the concrete completely and digging right down to the solid London clay.

Pat's mother, Sally (who lived with her daughter until she died) was a keen gardener too, and showed Pat how to make compost to improve the soil. As a result, the soil is now in tip-top condition, well-drained but fertile; so fertile in fact, that last season the broccoli reached eight feet high and Pat had to harvest it from the top of a step-ladder!

Today, within its framework of sculpture and hard landscaping, Pat's layout of pots and plants is constantly changing. Wedged in one shady corner next to the house

ADD SCULPTURAL PLANTS

It's not just sculpture that makes Pat's garden stand out – her plants have an architectural air too. Try these shapely beauties...

Byzantium gladioli:
H 45cm (18in), S 15cm (6in)

Allium christophii:
H 60cm (24in), S 15cm (6in)

Aquilegia vulgaris:
H 45cm (18in), S 15cm (6in)

Cyperus papyrus:
H 90cm (3ft), S 30cm (1ft)

Blue campanula, white erigeron and spiky sisyrinchium

is a small pool, flanked by camellias, and brightened by the cheerful creeping *Campanula portenschlagiana*, which pops up all over the garden, and is, according to Pat, virtually indestructible.

Around the pool stand all manner of pots which serve as a deterrent to Tigger the cat, who likes to forage for fish from the edge. 'He was so angry when I added some of the smaller pots the other day, that he bit me,' says Pat wryly. 'He likes to watch the fish, but unfortunately he also thinks they're quite tasty.'

Next to the pool, in the darkest corner against the house wall, is a tall mirror, strategically placed to reflect as much light as possible, but also to give the illusion that Pat's lush poolside vegetation continues indefinitely. More pots flank the wall, leading to a magnificent spiral water feature, sculpted by Pat some years ago.

Containers are also prominent on Pat's rooftop patio, where she grows a small range of vegetables, fruit and herbs. Notwithstanding the monster broccoli, she finally decided last year that the courtyard was too shaded for successful cropping, and so has transferred troughs of strawberries, peas,

Pat's sculpture integrates with her plants, here symbolising the spirit of the tree, among cotinus and campanula

Pan, the Greek god of nature

'All my sculptures are about nature and my relationship with it'

courgettes, carrots and sorrel to the roof garden, where they'll get more sunshine. Everything up here is (necessarily) in containers, including a row of what look like stylish zinc troughs. 'Actually they're old plastic toilet cisterns, supported on bricks to make raised beds!' she laughs. 'Mum and I used to plant our fruit and veg in anything we could get our hands on – barrels, old cut-down dustbins – even a plasterer's bath.' The carrots have special significance as they were planted by Pat's mum in the last year of her life. Pat has allowed them to set seed and is still growing carrots descended from the originals even today.

Many of Pat's plants are sown from seed and she's fond of experimenting to discover each plant's ideal growing conditions. 'I enjoy my garden enormously,' she says. 'It's the challenge of getting it right, just as it's the challenge of making a sculpture that's right. I just have to go on until I'm happy with it.'

Above: Pat's spiralling water feature adds a modern note

Left: Life imitates art – Tigger (left) eyes Pat's koi hungrily!

HOW TO AVOID SLUGS AND SNAILS

Pat has a number of trusted methods to cut down on the hordes of slugs and snails that attempt to infiltrate her many pots:

- **Encourage natural predators** such as frogs and hedgehogs into the garden, by gardening organically and keeping a pond. Pat says they help a great deal.

- **Encircle pots with copper bands,** such as Slug Stoppa Copper tape from Fito. The slugs and snails won't cross them, but you may need to re-stick the tapes occasionally.

- **Fill in the lip** around the top of any pot with a roll-over edge, otherwise it makes a good hiding place. Pat suggests using plasticine: roughen the surface of the pot, warm the plasticine slightly and fill in the gap, moulding it to the edge with your fingers.

City cloister

PASTEL REVIVAL From left to right a gorgeous display of violet *Geranium pratense 'Plenum Violaceum'*, with white daisies, hot pink Geranium 'Russell Pritchard' and lavender

Cristina Franchi has designed her London garden to create a haven filled with geraniums, lavender, clematis and grasses

A visit to Vita Sackville-West's home at Sissinghurst inspired Cristina Franchi to dream of becoming a garden designer. Only a teenager at the time, she was smitten with the gardening bug.

Initially, Cristina was pursuaded to consider other career options, and so became a social worker and enthusiastic amateur gardener. She settled down with her partner Peter and began raising a family, only to find her interest in garden design rekindled when they moved into their first family home at Elmsdale Road, East London.

The garden was a typical city one – long and narrow with a patch of grass and mean-looking flower beds. A concrete path led to the focal point of the garden – a rotary washing line! 'The garden was open and overlooked, but I wanted it to be a safe, enclosed space,' says Cristina.

'I was also keen to reflect the seasons, with the silhouettes of trees in winter, fresh, green buds in spring, and autumn foliage. My favourite look is traditional English, with pastel colours and romantic, exuberant planting.'

Cristina enrolled on an RHS garden design course at Capel Manor in north London and drew a scale plan of the existing plot. Firstly, the top part of the garden was designated as a

ABOUT CRISTINA'S GARDEN...

Where is the garden? London E17

How big is it? 21x6m

What's the soil type? Neutral London clay

Which direction does it face? North-west

Who do you share the garden with? My partner Peter, daughter Rose (16) and son Raphael (12), Hodge and Hebe the cats, Dusty the rabbit and Vespy the tortoise

Best gardening advice? From Christopher Lloyd, who once said, 'The best time to prune is when you have time to prune.' It's very true!

The flat round seedpods of honesty (*Lunaria annua*) complement lavender 'Munstead' perfectly – both are great plants for the classic English look

Delicate *Geranium pratense* 'Plenum Violaceum' steals the show from late May to August

relaxation and play area. Next to the house, she installed a small patio, separated from the garden by borders.

To create the illusion of width Cristina designed a circular lawn edged with brick so the shape would remain regardless of the punishment meted out to the grass by children and a rabbit. A line of conifers on one boundary was removed to increase light, and the hedge kept low to 'borrow' the view of a graceful corkscrew willow in a neighbouring garden.

For privacy they planted an autumn-flowering cherry (*Prunus subhirtella* 'Autumnalis') and a *Eucalyptus gunnii,* partly for Peter's Australasian origins, but mostly so their daughter Rose (then three years old) would have something to climb before she grew too old. Thirteen years on, and after regular judicious pruning, the gum tree dominates the top of the garden with its broad, sculptural branches.

The garden evolves from play area to plantswoman's paradise. Two small pools feature a variegated, less vigorous, form of the yellow flag iris (*Iris pseudacorus* 'Variegatus'), arum lily (*Zantedeschia aethiopica)*, and on the margins, bold-leafed *Ligularia dentata* 'Desdemona'. A sweeping circle of paving makes this small area feel deceptively spacious, leading across the garden and through a tunnel of foliage to a bench.

The tunnel is in fact a pergola of cordon-trained fruit trees (Cristina dreams of an

orchard!). Finally, tucked into the far corner of the plot, is the children's summerhouse, hidden from view.

Cristina believes in using good quality materials wherever possible. 'It's worth the investment, and the wait,' she says. 'If you buy cheap paving, it's never going to look right.'

Similarly, to achieve unity in planting, she uses a few large, bold plants rather than several small ones, which can look bitty. 'Look for a feeling of balance between the different shapes of plants and foliage,' she advises. 'A garden needs visual weight. For instance, a bold clump of ligularia 'The Rocket' is more effective than three or four different plants. Also, *Stipa arundinacea* looks so effective under the purple-leafed elder, that we've put in another for balance on the other side of the garden.' This places the grasses in partial shade – a reminder, says Cristina, that you need to consider not only what looks right but what will grow well in the space available.

The result is a fabulous garden that combines the best of everything, and it's not surprising that Cristina has now become a professional garden design consultant. She has created a family garden filled with pets and children, softened with lush areas of planting. Who could imagine a more soothing place to escape city life?

Dazzling *Clematis florida* 'Sieboldii' blooms in late summer (cut back after flowering)

The fragrant blue spikes of Lavandula angustifolia 'Munstead'

Cristina has customised her shed with coordinating stripes of navy and blue paint. A towering miscanthus in a pot, ivy and pale-pink *Geranium endressii* soften the look

CRISTINA'S TOP DESIGN TIPS

1 Draw a scale plan, measuring each boundary and plotting its features on graph paper before you start.

2 Decide how you want to use the garden and allocate areas for each activity. Use simple geometric shapes on the plan – big curves are less fussy.

3 Consider how to link and separate each area, for instance with paving, stepping stones, trellis and archways.

4 Address any 'problem' areas such as ugly views and wasted space.

5 Plan the planting on paper first, choosing species that suit your site, soil and how much time you're prepared to spend gardening. 'It's a good idea to balance evergreens with deciduous trees and shrubs for a variety of winter silhouettes,' advises Cristina.

This fabulous garden combines the best of everything – family, pets and lush planting

Circles of paving help create an impression of space

Sheila White's Bristol garden is a theatre for plants, with a few star players and a strong supporting cast – each with an important role to play.

SHEILA'S GARDEN

Where is the garden?
Bristol suburbs

How long did it take to create?
Three and a half years

How big is it?
10x9m (35x30ft)

What's the soil type?
Heavy clay

Which direction does it face? South

Shares garden with: Husband Eric

Favourite job: Deadheading!

As morning sunshine filters through Sheila's garden, it highlights the tall, arching stems of dierama with purple *Origanum laevigatum* 'Herrenhausen' below. White sedum, red impatiens, begonias and succulents nestle in pots at their feet

'My

garden theatre

Although Sheila White's sunny Bristol garden is barely four years old, it already has a sense of maturity which belies its tender years. As the seasons progress, black tulips spring forth like brazen exclamation marks through a carpet of hostas, soft grasses sway gently beside the geometric stems of acid-green euphorbia, and mauve clematis twines through golden-leaved *Lonicera nitida* 'Baggesen's Gold', trimmed into a puffy cloud formation.

Such marvels of pattern, shape and texture don't happen by accident – they've all been carefully planned by Sheila and her lawn-mowing, container-watering husband, Eric.

'I like to think of the garden as a theatre,' muses Sheila, 'with a few star players set off by a strong supporting cast. I'm the director and Eric's the caretaker – I couldn't have done this without him!'

It's a good analogy, given the way each 'cast member' plays a different role in making the garden look great all year round. And there's no room for show-off ham actors or sulky divas here!

Sheila's 'directorial debut' began about 16 years ago. 'I'd been gardening for years but decided to take an RHS course in horticulture at a local college, then followed it up with an intensive, week-long course in garden design. It was easy. Although I wasn't very good at drawing the 3D elevations, I found I could clearly visualise what each garden plan would look like in 10 years' time.

Plan for winter, then fill in

'Probably the best advice I got on the course was to plan for winter then fill in the gaps with plants for each of the other seasons,' Sheila says. 'Now I treat early and late summer separately, and make a point of visiting the garden centre all year round to see what looks good, when. But for me, flower colour isn't the main thing with plants. The main criteria is foliage. The flowers are lovely, but purely incidental.'

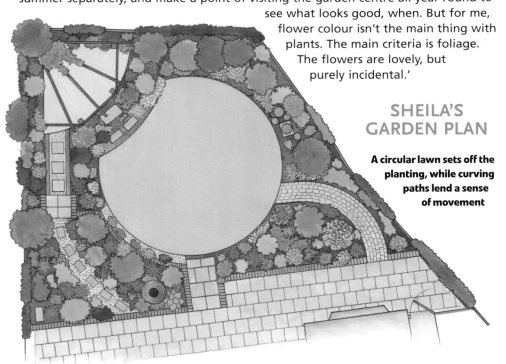

SHEILA'S GARDEN PLAN

A circular lawn sets off the planting, while curving paths lend a sense of movement

A neat stepping-stone path through lavender, phormium, white-flowered *Artemisia lactiflora* Guizhou Group and blue agapanthus

Above: Hot colours sizzle in this border, with lily 'Monte Negro', creamy-yellow *Anthemis tinctoria* 'Sauce Hollandaise' and red nasturtiums. Although her plants are positioned to form a colour wheel round the lawn, Sheila says flower colours are incidental to foliage

Left: Containers of dainty lobelia 'White Cascade', rich red pelargonium 'Tomcat' and *Pennisetum villosum* – with its squirrel-tail flowers – brighten up the patio. 'Touching the pennisetum is just lovely!' says Sheila

Right: Pinks and rich, greeny–blues are perfect partners in this sumptuous corner! *Blue Cerinthe major* and dark green euphorbia frame a mixture of lush grasses and pink-mauve *Verbena bonariensis.*

Below: In the gravel garden, red *Imperata cylindrica* 'Rubra' catches the sun, with *Briza media* in front and aromatic thyme between the paving slabs

'The best advice I got was to plan for winter, then fill in the gaps with plants for the other seasons'

Sheila's most successful foliage combinations include planting broad-leaved sage with spiky sisyrinchium and bushy euphorbia. 'I like to group exciting leaf shapes together – spiky plants such as phormiums help set off round-leaved ones such as nasturtiums, and small-leafed plants such as *Microbiota decussata* – a prostrate conifer.'

Grasses large and small, in black, blue, green and gold, are another favourite. 'I like designing with plants you can touch – the idea of pushing aside grasses and walking between them has always appealed to me. I have lots of them – floaty *Miscanthus sinensis* 'Malepartus' for height (which has reddish, feathery flowers fading to pale pink), arching, evergreen *Stipa arundinacea* (orange-bronze) and mound-forming *Pennisetum villosum* – which has soft,

squirrel-tail flowers, but isn't hardy in very cold winters so I keep it in a pot. Touching it is lovely!'

It's reassuring to learn that behind this sumptuous theatre of colour and texture lies a fair amount of hard work. 'The soil is solid clay,' says Sheila. 'Every plant we put in took about an hour – using bag after bag of our homemade compost, digging each hole 12-18 inches deep, removing the rocks, improving the soil and back-filling. It's a labour of love, though. And worth it – our plants have thrived while many of our neighbours' plants have died.'

Sheila is meticulous in her choice of plants, choosing only those specimens she knows will flourish in her clay soil, given their individual requirements for sun and shade. 'I also keep a

PLANTS IN DETAIL Some of Sheila's favourites for a long season of interest

Seedheads of Nectaroscordum siculum

Clematis durandii and Lonicera nitida

Allium cristophii

Thalictrum delavayi

Euphorbia myrsinites

'Plants are living things and deserve to look their best'

A wooden pergola on the east side of the garden gets plenty of late-afternoon sunshine. It's clothed in golden hop, sweet peas, late-flowering clematis, purple-leaved vitis and Virginia creeper (on the back fence). A neat clump of swaying grass Molina caerulea adds movement

record of all my plants in a card index file, together with seed packets and plant labels. I like to know what each plant is and how big it will grow. I use an old RHS diary to keep a note of when and where I bought them.

'I find gardening relaxing and very therapeutic – I can really get lost in it. I go out there for an hour and I'm gone all day! I can't sit down for very long – I always see something that needs my attention. Plants are living things which deserve to look their best. Besides, deadheading is so much more fun than housework!'

Janet and Ronan Sleep at their wisteria-covered home in Norfolk

Meet a gardener who rejected the instant fix approach in favour of growing for the future

Janet Sleep caught the gardening bug 25 years ago when she and husband Ronan moved into their first house, a little Edwardian terrace in Isleworth. Tending a garden for the first time opened her eyes to the potential of plants: 'It wasn't like housework,' she recalls. 'I planted a tiny thing in the garden and nature rewarded me by multiplying it. It was like being given sweets as a child. I began to look at plants properly for the first time and realised how incredibly beautiful they were, particularly in the way they change from day to day and week to week.'

The couple moved to their present garden, in Norfolk, during the harsh winter of 1978, when the snow lay on the ground for months, and then, when it finally departed, left a quagmire in its wake. The garden was open to the elements which, on the eastward side, meant winds blowing in directly from Siberia. With Ronan's help, Janet planted a series of

PHOTOGRAPHY: ANNE GREEN-ARMYTAGE

Seize the moment

Clematis 'Madame Julia Correvon' and weeping, silver–leaved pear, *Pyrus salicifolia* 'Pendula'

Yellow *Hypericum olympicum*, lime-green *Euphorbia nicaeensis*, *Lilium* 'Fata Morgana' and spiny-leaved *Helleborus sternii*

Although I like flowers, you have to look beyond that to shape and foliage colour, because flower is so fleeting

internal hedges to give enclosure, both as shelter and as a linking theme, creating different spaces which have taken on their own character over the years: formal, secret, courtyard, naturalistic and wild.

The northern part of the plot was largely old orchard that they grubbed up and removed, and at the far end Janet discovered all the good topsoil had been removed by the previous owners. Janet wanted to turn this area into a kitchen garden, so she imported 50 tons of topsoil, which she barrowed into position. Meanwhile, on the eastern side next to the house, they filled in a huge ditch, mechanically this time, into which, she says, the house was slowly sinking. This was then left to settle over a number of years, and has only recently been developed into a woodland walk and paved courtyard outside the kitchen window.

Janet worked full-time until three years ago when, after recovering from cancer, she decided to focus her attention more fully on the garden. 'I have lustful eyes when it comes to plants,' she says, smiling. 'I'm greedy for looking at things. And although I like flowers, you have to look beyond that to shape and foliage colour, because flower is so fleeting. So I've replaced a lot of shrub roses: they do their stuff in a big way but then they're a mess until you tidy them up, and after that they're boring.' Rose 'Charles de Mills' has therefore been turfed out in favour of a combination of *Kolkwitzia amabilis* 'Maradco' with its golden flush of foliage, and big bronzy *Phormium* 'Sundowner'. Similarly, purple-leaved *Cercis canadensis* 'Forest Pansy', and evergreen *Arbutus unedo*, the strawberry tree, have replaced rose 'Fantin-Latour'.

Eryngiums, euphorbias and bergenias are also high on Janet's list of must-haves, for their long season of interest and for their form and texture. She maintains bergenias have been unjustly slighted in recent years; a favourite with Gertrude Jekyll, there are now new cultivars which have immense glossy leaves, and some that are slightly hairy, such as *Bergenia ciliata*. 'It's texture

as much as anything else,' she says. 'If a plant says "touch me", then I must have it. Even the eryngiums, although you regret it when you do!'

A sense of structure runs through the planting, with naturalistic, flowing borders punctuated by box pyramids, statuary and topiary yew, the latter grown from plants self-seeded from the hedging, which Janet couldn't bear to throw away. This eye for structure is also evident in the layout of the garden: sheltered courtyards and secret, tucked-away places contrast with vistas of sweeping lawns and borders, glimpsed

Eryngium 'Jos Eijking' (sea holly) provides spiky marbled foliage as well as flowers

Long-lasting *Knautia macedonica* provides random dots of colour all summer

After flowering, allium 'Globemaster' provides large, spherical seedheads

Hardy *Dactylorhiza foliosa* (marsh orchid) flowers in late spring and early summer

Verbascum olympicum forms rosettes of large, grey-white, woolly leaves

In June, *Allium schubertii* bears up to 50 small, starry flowers on each stem

Right: Clipped box pyramids *(Buxus sempervirens)* frame the view from the garden room courtyard to the gravel garden

Pink-flowered, evergreen *Geranium maderense* blooms from late winter to late summer, enjoying the shelter of the greenhouse

through archways cut into golden philadelphus or draped with vines. 'I don't like island beds,' she says firmly. 'I much prefer sweeping borders that join up. But I do like seeing through a border from two sides – it adds an extra dimension to the garden and makes it seem bigger. So there are pathways going behind the borders, and in places I've deliberately left holes so you can see through them, and used stepping stones to make convenient paths and circular routes.'

Janet is particularly aware of the play of light in the garden, a subject which forms one of the cornerstones of a book she has just completed, *The Designing Gardener*. Noel Coward, commenting on the East Anglian landscape in his play, *Private Lives*, wrote: 'Very flat, Norfolk'. Although this is considered a little extreme by its inhabitants, moving here has made Janet more aware of seasonal changes in light, as she now experiences it for longer than she did living in a city. 'Having become aware of plant shape and form, I now realise that it's the interaction between form and light that provides the interest,' she explains. 'Back-lighting instantly turns a boring coloured picture into a stained glass window. *Cercis canadensis* 'Forest Pansy' has wonderfully red leaves, and because of its position you can see the light coming through them from early morning until late afternoon, transforming the dark red into a glowing ruby port.' Boundary hedges around the garden are kept at a level which allows the low sunlight of long summer evenings to flood in, creating theatrical pools

of light while topiary casts monstrous shadows on the smooth lawns.

But the garden has not been without its problems. The old orchard left Janet with a legacy of honey fungus which proved a real challenge, killing off two ancient and statuesque walnut trees. Having decided they needed to come out completely, she broke the news to Ronan who, heroically, with only a hand winch and a little ingenuity, got both trees out, roots and all, while Janet, anxious for the safety of the house, cowered behind the garage.

She replanted initially with hollies and other native shrubs that have some resistance to the disease, and also used fast-maturing plants such as ceanothus, which could do their thing before the fungus struck again. But more recently she has risked planting a *Cornus kousa chinensis*, a form of dogwood with beautiful white bracts which is very slow to come to maturity. 'So far', she says philosophically, 'it has survived, even though it sits right on the site of one of the walnuts.

As you get older you've got to seize every moment. I'm very aware of that clock ticking, so I take each day as it comes and try to enjoy everything, because life's not worth wasting.'

Right: Janet uses grasses, such as this *Stipa gigantea*, for form and texture as well as the way their appearance alters according to the light. Hairy-leaved *Phlomis russeliana*, with yellow flowers from May to September, provides textural contrast in front of a small conifer

Sun Ho.
Long Melford

This shady terrace tinkles with the magical sound of a fountain, framed by pink *Geranium endressii, Sisyrinchium striatum* and neat roundels of clipped box

MAUREEN'S GARDEN

Soil type: Acid – pH4.5 to 6.5

Position: South east-facing

Size: Third of an acre

Time spent in garden: About 15-16 hours a week not including pottering

Has been here: 20 years

Organic?: Not entirely. I spray for blackspot and mildew

Top tip: Walk round daily, to keep an eye on what needs doing in advance

Enter the secret garden

Take inspiration from Maureen Thompson's fabulous walled garden and find out how to achieve privacy and beauty.

PHOTOGRAPHY: ANNE GREEN-ARMYTAGE

Behind the busy main street of Long Melford, in Suffolk, lies one of its best-kept secrets. Step through an unassuming doorway squeezed between cottage and shop-front, into a tiny forecourt, past a wooden gate, and suddenly the traffic noise dims to a murmur and the sound of birdsong and the musical splash of a fountain take over.

This is Sun House, the magical garden of Maureen Thompson, and her late husband John, who moved here 20 years ago, enchanted by the higgledy-piggledy roofscape (dating back to 1471), and the potential of a derelict garden bounded by picturesque old walls. 'It was the site which gave us the encouragement to make it what it is now – that was the canvas we had to work on,' says Maureen. 'I think it would have been more difficult in a bleak place without defined edges.'

Surrounded on three sides by the house, and overshadowed by a magnificent mature *Robinia pseudoacacia*, the fountain courtyard opens out onto green lawn, flanked by curving borders which lead the eye to the figure of a white lady at the end of the garden (inset). 'We got her

An old stone arch frames the view to the golden border, containing blue-green hosta 'Frances Williams' behind golden sedge *Carex elata* 'Aurea'. On the far right is the yellow-leaved, evergreen shrub, *Choisya ternata* 'Sundance'

131

These informal borders of pink *Gladiolus byzantinus*, blue geranium (both on the left) and blue *Iris sibirica* lead to a clump of red poppies and the hidden wildlife pond

Fragrant roses and informal poppies contrast with neatly clipped box and old brickwork

Trimmed topiary spirals complement the box border edging

The mauve heads of *Allium cristophii*, red rose 'Madame Isaac Pereire', pink, myrrh-scented rose 'Constance Spry' and spires of pink foxgloves thrive in sun against this old brick wall

from a local shop for £50, as she has a chip on her back,' remembers Maureen. 'John had just had an operation and we had to drive round with her in the back of the car for some time until a travelling salesman came to the door and was able to help me unload her!'

The statue reclines beneath a silver-leaved weeping pear (*Pyrus salicifolia* 'Pendula'), with the rounded foliage of bergenias at her feet. The pear has been trimmed back so she's visible from the house, making a strong focal point. 'There wasn't a plant in the garden when we put her in; we planned the beds round her. I think it's important to find points of focus from the house that give you pleasure: if you're washing up and you look out of the window, your eye has to be drawn somewhere.'

Although Maureen denies having designed the garden formally, her sense of structure is evident throughout, from the spiral topiary in stylish terracotta pots, to the

mosaic sun motif in an ornate shell 'folly' (which, she says, was created purely to hide the compost heap). In particular, her eye for combining plant shapes and colours lifts the garden from being merely a collection of interesting plants into a dramatic entity, spiky sisyrinchiums contrasting with mounds of tumbling shrub roses, and spires of white foxgloves shooting skywards into the graceful foliage of the small tree, *Betula pendula* 'Youngii'. 'I look for a few visually strong plants,' she says. 'And I think verticals matter tremendously. Irises and sisyrinchiums, crocosmias, *Melianthus major:* these give you wonderfully strong shapes and then you can fit in the "pretty bits" around them.'

Her favourite colour schemes are those she finds most restful and calming: the pink shades of clematis and

Right: Old-fashioned roses, including fragrant, pale pink 'Mme Alfred Carrière', lead the eye to a stately lion's head wall fountain, framed by fragrant honeysuckle and hosta 'Happiness'

Far right: The handsome bearded iris, 'Blue Rhythm'

Rose 'Souvenir du Docteur Jamain' starts to bloom just as spring-flowering *Clematis macropetala* 'Markham's Pink' finishes

Cheerful pansies and variegated ivy cascade from an old stone urn

old-fashioned roses, and the soft yellow and silver of alchemilla, artemisia and *Stachys byzantina*. Hot colours are completely banished from the vicinity of the house, but further up the garden they find space near the little wildlife pond: sizzling red crocosmias are teamed with green-yellow *Euphorbia wallichii* and coppery *Euphorbia griffithii* 'Dixter', and later in the season with the bright red dahlia, 'Bishop of Llandaff'.

Maureen attributes her enthusiasm for plants at least in part to what she calls a universal earth mother urge... 'In the autumn I want to put them to bed and in spring I can't wait for the first flower to come out, to tend and cosset it,' she explains. 'I think the cycle of the seasons has a great pull.' She also sets great store in stopping and staring, looking at flowers in close-up. 'When you're busy as a gardener there are so many jobs piled up and waiting, but if you actually take the time to sit back on your heels and look at the face of a viola, or the inside of a shrub rose, they really do look extraordinary.'

Small wonder, then, that when the opportunity arose to buy a small corner of her neighbour's garden, Maureen jumped at it. 'For many years, when I was pruning my roses on the step ladder, I used to look over the wall at this curious dog-leg of my neighbour's garden and think it would make a wonderful secret garden. I'd always loved the idea

of having a secret garden because of the children's book by Frances Hodgson Burnett.' So, in the face of fierce competition from other would-be purchasers, she sold her entire antique glass collection to secure the plot.

The result is a tiny secluded parterre, quartered into formal box-edged beds which overflow with her favourite flowers. Snug within its four high walls, the little courtyard is an object lesson in stylish use of space: the summerhouse with its plain stuccoed columns flanked by box spirals and covered in climbers; the lion's head wall-fountain, underplanted with hosta 'Happiness', which is echoed at the other end of the box-edged pathway by the same hosta below a Grecian flower-lady. And throughout, a joyful abundance of old-fashioned roses, on the walls intertwined with clematis and honeysuckle, and in the beds tumbling over the box edging and vying for attention with alliums and irises.

Maureen feels the secret garden was worth every penny. 'This is my favourite part of the whole garden. There's such a sense of secrecy, security and privacy. I come here and sit in the summerhouse and just switch off. The outside world fades into the distance. I think gardens are incredibly therapeutic, and if you get the chance to sit in peace in a place like this, it has to be the nearest thing to paradise.'

Walled gardens have privacy and secrecy

Maureen loves her secret garden most
of all – with blousy pink rose 'Madame
Isaac Pereire' framing the path

Big ideas in

Theo Stanning's garden in Ely, Cambridgeshire, inspires with its skilful use of a wide array of plants

a small city

THEO'S GARDEN

Aspect: North-west facing

Soil types: Friable sandy loam

Size: Half an acre

How long have you lived here:
15 years

Salvia sylvestris **is a reliable plant that blooms for many months through summer**

'When designing a garden, use plants as accents, to add structure and to link different areas together'

Is it my interest in plants, or just sheer nosiness that draws me to visit other people's gardens? Whatever it is, snooping around someone else's patch makes a great day out and always gives me ideas to try at home. Ely in Cambridgeshire may be famous for its cathedral, but it's also home to a great mix of gardens large and small.

I chose Theo Stanning's house, because I was intrigued by its description in the Yellow Book - the paperback which lists all the gardens open under the National Gardens Scheme. Brief in the extreme - designed ½ acre garden with interesting and unusual plants - it intrigued me and I wanted to know more. The word

'designed' indicates planning, which is one area where I can improve while the mention of 'interesting and unusual plants' made me anxious to have a nose around. No two gardens are ever the same and I enjoy seeing how different gardeners use their plots - sharing ideas is a great learning experience. I also love discovering new plants and testing my knowledge on those I should know, but can't remember!

Belmont House is quite a grand residence with a curving gravel drive and large bay windows. Despite this it has a friendly, welcoming air and sits comfortably among mature landscaped gardens. The colourful, well-structured borders

Theo dresses a pot of lavenders with gravel

leaves and stems. A golden hop scrambles between the plants, creating a visual link that draws your eye from one end to the other. The purple leaves of *Lysimachia ciliata* 'Firecracker' are a great foil and, with a dark-leaved elder and *Physocarpus opulifolius* 'Diabolo', create a wonderful, dark, backdrop.

'Where do you get your inspiration?', I enquire. 'I spent my childhood in Kent,' says Theo, 'and Sissinghurst is one of the most wonderful gardens. It's captivating'.

'I've made mistakes over the years, though' she continues, 'mainly because I over-indulge in certain plants. But I never get rid of anything just because it's common. Some really common plants are the backbone of my garden'.

One plant that stands proud is *Halimiocistus wintonensis* 'Merrist Wood Cream', which has stunning creamy-yellow flowers with maroon centres. It's ideal for a sunny position in well-drained soil and has an Award of Garden Merit from the RHS.

A wide herbaceous border curves down the right hand side mirroring that on the left and helps the garden feel balanced. The scale and proportion of all the garden features are essential in creating an effective design and Theo's made sure the borders are deep enough to offset the imposing house beyond. I'm drawn by the border's vibrant mix of colour, with lupins, campanula and honesty are all at their peak in midsummer and competing for attention. There are no subtle colour schemes here, rather a cottage-style mix of perennials that shows no restraint.

are packed with perennials but there are enough evergreens to hold your interest all year round. However, it's in the detail that the garden really comes alive.

'I love working with plants and always have done,' explains Theo as we start walking round, 'In fact I enjoyed it so much I trained in horticulture, looking at both plants and garden design. It's an area I've loved working in in the past and I'm endeavouring to try my hand at it again in the near future'.

From the large, weathered terrace behind the house, the garden opens up before us, each aspect framed by the rustic wooden pergola, which provides shelter

from the sun. Her gently curving borders are chock-a-block with shrubs and herbaceous perennials, while the trees in the boundary create a vibrant green tapestry behind. Initially, it feels as if the whole garden's open to our gaze, but I sense hidden depths and twisting pathways among the undergrowth.

'When designing a garden, use plants as accents, to add structure and to link different areas together,' Theo advises. Yellow is one theme she's used effectively with phlomis, asters, ligularia 'Desdemona', euphorbias, astrantia, epimediums, grasses and even lilies - with striking turkscap-like flowers - contributing golden flowers,

Halimiocistus wintonensis 'Merrist Wood Cream' thrives in sun

Again, leafy shrubs provide a textured backdrop against which the perennials can strut their stuff. 'This is *Viburnum henryi*', she says indicating a large shrub so covered in white flowers you can barely see the leaves. I'm not usually a fan of viburnum, but this has such an abundance of blooms, it reminds me of a little of pyracantha in May. Theo obviously prefers fairly loose planting schemes, though they all have a well-structured central core. There's not a great deal of formality, no classic rose garden or clipped hedging. 'Roses are no good in this garden', says Theo, 'they need too much feeding'.

A plant with leaves like those of *Clematis montana* and tiny, starry, white flowers also catches my eye. 'That's *Clematis recta* 'Purpurea'', says Theo to my enquiry. 'It isn't very disciplined but isn't it's foliage lovely. I don't prune it - just tie it in a little because it's very exuberant.'

The soft, powder-blue flowers of nigella appear like wisps of smoke among the other low-growing plants, testament to Theo's ability to grow from seed. 'I love sowing and taking cuttings. I've grown a brugmansia from Nairobi, a loquat from southern Ireland and an eccremocarpus from a seed pod.

As one of the older town houses in Ely, there's a superb view of the cathedral,

'You'll find ideas develop as your plants grow. Be disciplined but always maintain a sense of curiosity'

especially if you climb on top of the old air-raid shelter. The bunches of cerise flowers of *Rhodohypoxis baurii* make it worth the scramble, even if you have to get down on your knees in the undergrowth to admire them.

A self-seeded *Cephalaria gigantea* stands tall in the centre of a border at the end of the garden, alongside the yellow-flowered foxglove, *Digitalis lutea*. 'I'm fascinated by the idea of a gravel garden with poppies, violas and even paeonies. I'd like to clear these beds and have a bit more discipline, using large drifts of plants. It would be great if I could make the garden easier to manage'.

Theo then leads me around the back of the borders. These paths meander gently and are cool as they're shaded by

overhanging plants. It's lovely walking among taller plants. Seeing them close up and immersing yourself among them gives you a completely different perspective.

Theo offers some advice. 'Grow what you've got well and keep an eye on everything. A garden is an ongoing project and you shouldn't let it daunt you. Take your knowledge as building blocks and consolidate'.

I ask which is Theo's favourite. 'This is the thistle *Silybum marianum*', she replies. 'Its variegated leaves look wonderful with the white flowers of dictamnus and the velvety, silver foliage of *Salvia aethiopis*'.

As I prepare to leave, Theo offers one last piece of advice. 'You'll find ideas develop as your plants grow. Be disciplined but always maintain a sense of curiosity'.

'A garden is an ongoing project and you shouldn't let it daunt you'

Right: The packed greenhouse provides plants for the garden

Left: A cool, fragrant border links the garden and house

Below: Summer flowers spill from the packed borders

Above: *Dictamnus albus,* **the burning bush, has foliage that gives off flammable oils in hot weather. Light it for a party trick or just enjoy its glaucous foliage and beautiful flowers**

Jennifer's midsummer garden bursts with colour from creamy climbing roses, lavender-blue nepeta and yellow sisyrinchium

Jennifer Wood knew little about gardening when she moved to her half-acre Rutland plot, and yet the immaculate borders and rose garden have flourished under her care. Find out how a novice can become a great gardener...

'I was a novice...

142

now I'm a plantaholic'

A star of the early summer garden, pink and papery *Cistus purpureus* (AGM)

'For the first few years, I tried to keep it exactly the same. But when I realised I could move plants, my confidence grew...'

Taking on an established garden and making it your own is always a challenge, but it can be quite daunting for a complete beginner. Throwing off the old order requires not only confidence and guidance, but patience too, while waiting to see if the new schemes fail or flourish.

'For the first few years, I tried to keep it exactly the same,' says Jennifer Wood, of Rutland. 'Then I enlisted the help of my late father-in-law who was a very good gardener. Once he told me what the plants were and how to look after them, my confidence grew. Especially when I realised that if I planted something in the wrong place, I could always move it.

'Although I did keep the formal structure of the garden, I decided to personalise it by softening it with plants such as catmint that spill over the border edges,' she explains. A quick glance at some old photographs and Jennifer's influence is clear – the planting style has changed completely from ordered lines of hyacinths and tulips to old scented roses, flowering and variegated shrubs and drifts of cottage flowers.

'Once the children grew up I started to steal from the lawn and reshape the borders, making them deeper and wider – not just for more plants but because I wanted to make the planting look more natural,' says Jennifer. 'The

HOME TRUTHS

What was it like to take on an established garden? Horrific! I knew nothing about gardening then, but now I'm county organiser for the National Gardens Scheme in Rutland.

What was the first thing you got rid of? All the orange roses. I love roses but hate orange. Then I got rid of the washing line which ran the length of the garden, and most of the conifers too, which I loathe.

How did you start making the garden your own? By reshaping the borders and planting climbers – lots of clematis – and making more herbaceous beds.

What advice would you give other readers taking on an established garden? Don't be afraid to plant things and move them, but do keep a record of where and what they are. Of course, a garden is never finished and new projects mean I'm learning all the time.

What was your biggest mistake? Getting rid of the greenhouse... My husband was furious!

Jennifer's Pool Garden resembles a Provençal courtyard, using golden walls and gravel to set off yellow santolina, geraniums and hebes

thing I love most is when plants mingle together, creating their own combinations.'

Look around the garden and you can see examples of these 'minglers' – sociable plants that love nothing more than getting together with their neighbours – all over the place. Roses and conifers play host to twining climbers such as clematis and golden hop, while at ground level herbaceous plants such as astrantias, red centranthus (valerian) and geraniums (cranesbill) form a revelling mass. For example, *Geranium psilostemon* (AGM) and the lime-green leaves and vivid magenta flowers of *Geranium* 'Ann Folkard' (AGM) have filled their space at ground level and are now climbing up to canoodle with the roses behind.

'The idea was to make the borders so chock-a-block with flowers there'd be no room for weeds,' says Jennifer, who by her own admission can't resist seeking out and buying new plants. 'It's got to the stage where I'm running out of planting space! But the good thing is, I feel that it's become more self-maintaining. It could almost look after itself for a season or two.'

Although the planting style has become more relaxed, the original stone walls – a soft buttermilk yellow – remain. These help break up the garden into smaller pockets, each with its own planting and atmosphere. The largest is The Pool Garden which looks as though it has been magically transported from Provence. Here the ground is swathed in golden gravel, chosen for its warm ochre colour to complement the walls and allow sun-loving plants such as rock rose, macleaya and thyme to grow through.

Enclosed gardens like this are ideal for holding scent, so here the walls are adorned with rambling roses such as the fragrant, creamy-white 'Bobbie James' and jasmine. Sound is trapped, too, so this part of the garden has great tranquillity, enhanced by the echo of tinkling water from a handsome lion's head fountain.

PERSONAL TOUCHES

A sundial is the perfect focal point for a walkway, or the centre of your lawn.

The quiet tinkle of water from a lion's head fountain adds a timeless feel.

For a truly unique touch, add sculpture. This piece is by Jennifer's daughter Rachel

'The thing I

Soften up the planting scheme by planting 'minglers' such as red and pink valerian with alchemilla mollis – just don't forget to dead head

love most is when plants mingle together and make their own natural combinations'

Treat established borders to some fresh new colour combinations

Jennifer likes to link plants in colour trios – matching the foliage colour of one plant with the flowers of another. Favourites include:

Clematis 'Arabella'

Rose 'Heather Austin'

Hebe andersonii.

Although Jennifer's garden was originally quite formal in layout, plants such as nepeta (catmint) have helped relax the edges.

Other planting ideas include using 'minglers' – sociable plants that snuggle up to their neighbours, such as astrantias, centranthus and geraniums – this is *Geranium oxonianum* 'Wargrave Pink' (AGM).

To get to The Pool Garden you walk through a densely planted corridor of roses, romneya, clematis and *Crambe cordifolia* (AGM). Just as you think you've reached the bottom of the garden, a view opens up of a large lawn surrounded by flower beds, elegantly framed by the trunk and branches of a cherry tree. 'This is the bit of the garden that I'm most proud of,' says Jennifer. 'It's such a surprise to visitors who think they've seen the whole thing!'

But it's Jennifer's mastery of colour that has given her garden such a distinctive and individual stamp. 'I come from a family of art lovers and like to arrange the views and borders like a painting, linking different plants together by colour,' she explains.

Jennifer's 'plant pictures' concentrate on the juxtaposition of coloured foliage and flowers. A good example is her use of yellow-leaved *Spiraea japonica* 'Goldflame' (AGM) with furry green leaves and acid yellow-green flowers of alchemilla, while the rose-pink spiraea flowers reflect the candy-coloured blooms of *Geranium oxonianum* 'Wargrave Pink' (AGM).

Another planting trio is based around the variegated shrub *Rhamnus alaternus* 'Argenteovariegata' (AGM), its silver-edged leaves complementing a huge stand of long-flowering, pearly *Astrantia major* with rose-red centres that match the petals of clematis 'Madame Julia Correvon' (AGM) scrambling over the top.

Although Jennifer has changed much of the garden, she thinks it's important to know when to stop. 'It's always tempting to rip out plants you dislike when you first arrive but I'm actually glad I resisted chopping down the leylandii hedge, which I hated.' The stone walls, trees and hedges offer protection from the often harsh winds that blow up across the Chater Valley.

'The wind, combined with the dry, sandy loam, means that some plants such as delphiniums and lupins just won't grow without support, so I stick to plants such as hebes that I know will thrive.' And thrive they do. One particularly outstanding plant sits next to the gravel drive – a *Hebe andersonii*, which has become a giant fountain of flowers some 2m (6ft 6in) tall, with cascades of pendent blue and white flowers from top to toe. It loves its sunny position, sheltered by a wall, and is rarely out of flower, even having one or two right through the winter.

Jennifer's most recent addition is a kitchen garden – a rectangular patch divided diagonally with vegetables on one side, lawn on the other. 'The dogs follow us everywhere, so I had to incorporate a romping area nearby which they couldn't ruin!' says Jennifer.

To keep aphids off the veg, husband David grows

Left: Jennifer has introduced woodland paths through *Vinca major* 'Variegata' (AGM) and *Alchemilla mollis* (AGM).

Above: Jennifer had a brainwave for this shady corner: use it to hide the compost bin

Left: Protect precious plants from sniffing Labradors with willow hurdles!

TAKING ON AN ESTABLISHED PLOT

Here's how to banish the garden ghosts from your established plot.

1 Map the existing garden through the seasons so you can see at a glance, on paper, where each plant is and where those bulbs are hiding! Test the soil's pH and note all the shady and sunny areas. Use RHS reference books from the library to help identify any new or unusual plant varieties.

2 Assess the garden's year-round structure – in particular, which plants still look interesting in winter? Which way does the patio face? Can you walk round the garden freely to enjoy it? Do any walls or fences need repairing?

3 Decide which elements you like and want to keep, and those to get rid of. Before getting the saw out (!), check the tree/feature isn't useful, for either shelter or privacy.

4 Sit and wait. Sometimes something new and wonderful will emerge from the soil...

5 Overlay a sketch of your dream garden onto the existing garden map. Divide it into manageable chunks and don't be afraid to move new plants if the original position didn't work.

marigolds as companion plants to entice aphid-eating hoverflies.

Apart from the four dogs, Jennifer also shares her garden with the family's two cats and the artworks made by her sculptor daughter, Rachel. And then there are the visitors who come scouting for ideas when it's open under the National Gardens Scheme. 'Last year, the lady we bought the house from stopped by and saw what I had done... To my great relief, she loved it!'

Gardening should always be fun and a well-placed bench is the perfect place to relax and enjoy the fruits of your labours

Natural style

Take inspiration from nature, by layering your plants and letting the flowers mingle across the seasons. Ailsa and David Jackson have created the perfect example

Almost translucent, the flowers of poppies such as 'Cedric Morris' are spell-binding though transient

When Ailsa Jackson talks about plants – whether it's her collection of double geraniums or 'Mother of Pearl' poppies – her enthusiasm is so catching, it makes you want to grow them, too. She admits to having 'caught the gardening bug about 24 years ago' – but it's got to be the most contagious strain we've ever seen!

And, with more than 2500 different plant varieties on show in her one-acre, clay soil garden in Ashby-de-la-Zouch, Leicestershire, it's amazing she has the energy to talk about them at all!

'I like my borders to be full,' she explains. 'Plants grow best in company and if you plant in layers you can squeeze more in and have plenty of colour for longer.'

This clever layering technique refers to the way you can combine plants with different seasons of interest in more or less the same space, planting them close and growing

A rustic post is a great setting for a late-flowering clematis such as 'Jackmanii' (AGM) which has velvety, dark-purple blooms. It will reach 3m in height but can be cut back hard in spring. Shade its roots from the sun

Ailsa's favourite plants

Top left Allow the poppy 'Muriel Brown' to self-seed across the garden and it will add a natural feel to the planting

Top right Make the most of your hardy geraniums by cutting them back after their first flush of flowers. Feed and water them well and they may well bloom again

Bottom left Although Ailsa's collection of primroses is best enjoyed blooming in spring, *Primula florindae*, the giant cowslip, flowers well into summer

Bottom right Crocosmia are excellent plants for late summer colour with funnel-shaped flowers in many fiery shades. Plant them in moderately fertile soil in moist but well-drained soil. They love a sunny position and benefit from some protection. Divide older clumps in spring

bulbs up through the middle.

'The year starts with dog's tooth violets *(Erythronium dens-canis)* and snowdrops. When they've finished flowering, out come the primulas, then the double geraniums, and then summer-flowering plants such as Jacob's ladder and asters,' says Ailsa.

Planting in this way also gives shelter to those plants that don't like hot summer sun. 'We struggle with primroses because of the heat, but they love it in the dappled shade of other plants. It keeps them cool.'

With such packed planting, supplements of food and water are essential and each winter a generous layer of compost and horse manure compost from the garden centre is piled between the plants, both to sustain them through the growing season and to help the soil store extra water.

This has been the key to success with Ailsa's 100-strong National Plant Collection of primroses, and also her delicate Himalayan poppies *(Meconopsis betonicifolia)*. 'They're both greedy plants and enjoy shady moist conditions,' says Ailsa. 'Usually if I buy a plant and it doesn't do well I give it three chances, trying it in three places, then if it still doesn't grow, that's it. I'll not try again. But,' she laughs, 'the meconopsis is so beautiful I just kept trying till I got it right!'

Ailsa contracted her 'gardening bug' while buying a primrose from a mail order catalogue. 'It was a double yellow and I loved it so much I kept it indoors and in no time at all the central heating had killed it. But I was determined to have more and I learnt how to grow them along the way. I particularly love the doubles and the Jack-in-the-green primroses, but all of them are wonderful,' raves Ailsa.

> **'Usually, if I buy a plant and it doesn't do well, I give it three chances to grow'**

NOVEL PLANTING IDEAS

Primroses aren't the only plants Ailsa grows. To one side of the house a thin path is perfumed with the scent of roses and winds its way through banks of foxgloves, cranesbills and campanulas. Unlike conventional planting schemes, here there are as many tall plants at the front as there are at the back. 'I like to mix heights all the way through the border as I think it looks more natural, and the plants seem to like it too,' Ailsa laughs.

Another border, flanking a drive, is chock-a-block with the cascading orange pompons of *Buddleja globosa,* coniferous *Cryptomeria japonica* and dozens of scrambling astrantias, large leathery-leaved ligularias and white *Anemone japonica*.

Ailsa points out some of her favourites along the way. First there's the double red Welsh poppy, *Meconopsis cambrica* 'Muriel Brown', then the white, paper-petalled hybrids of *Viola cornuta*, flowering from spring until late June, when Ailsa shears them back to encourage another flush of flowers in late summer. Then there are the 'Mother of Pearl' poppies in pale shades of white and grey. 'I sow them every year in the borders and when they come into flower I pull out any reds to keep the strain pure,' she explains.

Ailsa is happiest working in her garden

HOME TRUTHS

Which gardener most inspires you? I've always been spurred on by the garden designer Marjory Fish. She said there should be a flower for every day of the year. It's what I aimed to do in my garden and now I've achieved it

Which gardening books can't you live without? The Pan Garden Plant series. I've got several volumes including *Early Perennials, Late Perennials* and *Bulbs*

Which garden most inspires you? Lambrook Manor, in Somerset, which used to belong to Marjory Fish

How long do you spend gardening each day? From nine in the morning until dark. I hate housework!

Have you any great gardening advice? Get out and take cuttings. I love propagating and use heat and mist regularly. I take cuttings non-stop from March until October

Any on-going projects? There's always something happening. At the moment we're creating an oval-shaped border

What are you planning to plant? There's going to be everything under the sun! Hardy orchids are my latest thing, including many of the British natives

Any recurring problems? I still have a problem with bindweed (convolvulus) despite painting it with weedkiller – it keeps popping up everywhere

Deadheading is much more fun than being indoors. By cutting off faded flowers early, Ailsa stimulates more blooms

On the other side of the drive there's a tall beech hedge. 'It's seen some surgery... and it'll see a bit more, too!' laughs Ailsa, who leaves all the mowing, hedge-trimming and tree-care to her husband, David. Behind the hedge is a quarter-acre plot that has become a mini-arboretum. 'It makes us laugh when people call it that,' says David. 'It's such a grand term and not us at all.'

The collection contains unusual varieties such as *Castanea sativa* 'Variegata' – a variegated sweet chestnut which has striking white-edged leaves – and a *Pinus coulteri* conifer, famous for its pine cones bigger than pineapples!

'I'd been looking for that tree for years,' recalls David, 'and finally I tracked one down at the Harrogate Flower Show. Garden centres don't stock rarer plants as they're too slow and fiddly to get a fast turnover. If you want something different you've got to be prepared to travel, or join the specialist plant societies.'

CANOPY DELIGHTS

Larger trees include a semi-mature blue cedar, a silver-leaved eucalyptus and half a dozen birch and cornus. These are used as 'nurse trees', under whose protective canopy David plants younger arrivals. 'I plant them close so there's one for interest now and one up-and-coming to replace it,' he explains. 'It also gives the young tree protection from the wind.'

This shelter is essential as the Jacksons' garden can be terrifically windy. When the couple first moved here in 1976, the garden comprised just 17 fruit trees, all blowing onto their sides. 'We struggled, it was so gusty,' remembers David. 'The first thing we had to do was plant hedges and windbreaks before we could grow anything else.'

In the lea of a birch and ash windbreak, Ailsa has dug a series of beds and shoe-horned plants into them. Many have bright, variegated foliage – to visually lift the shadows cast by the trees – such as red-stemmed *Cornus alba* 'Sibirica', *Symphytum uplandicum* 'Variegatum' and the variegated *Polemonium caeruleum* 'Brise d'Anjou'.

Standing clear of the dappled shade, a 'Kiftsgate' rose clambers over a pergola, while all around lie plants whose labels read like the catalogue from a rare plant nursery. 'Anything new and I'm there,' laughs Ailsa infectiously. And it's true – everywhere there's evidence of this plantaholicism. Ailsa has 25 different varieties of double geranium, including the lavender-blue *Geranium pratense* 'Plenum Caeruleum' and the later-flowering 'Plenum Violaceum', whose violet-blue blooms have centres shaped like a rosette. They're so gorgeous it's easy to see how her garden's become a paradise. 'If I get one plant from a family, I'm not happy until I've got them all!'

HOW TO CREATE A MORE NATURAL LOOK

Visit any woodland or hedge-fringed meadow and you'll see how plants naturally grow in random layers. To recreate the effect at home, group your plants informally, combining varieties with different heights and flowering seasons.

Above: The natural look in a pot. Trailing, lime green helichrysum contrasts beautifully with evergreen perennials such as this rich purple heuchera

Left: Achieve the natural look by mixing early- and late-flowering shrubs and perennials. Here, pink rose 'The Fairy' grows among yellow anthemis, while pale poppies add an ethereal quality as they shimmer above the border

A home away from home

American expat Anne Huntingdon has spent 20 years creating a three-acre English garden with a twist in rural Northamptonshire.

The rose garden takes intensive effort but rewards so well in summer

As she opens her garden regularly, Anne has a mixture of plants in terracotta pots, bringing those in flower to the front of the display

America may be bigger but it's not always better. Well, not in Anne Huntingdon's eyes. Born in upstate New York, Anne moved to England over 20 years ago when she married. 'There's lots of snow where I grew up, which kills everything. It's much better here – you can grow so much more. My father still doesn't believe me when I tell him that we don't have to prune roses hard in winter', she laughs.

'You'd never guess now that I hated gardening as a child,' says Anne as we settle down with a cup of tea and look out through her French windows. She gives me a mischievous smile. 'But I remember being in awe of my grandmother and she had a large garden near Niagara Falls'. Gardening must be in the genes somewhere.

'I moved here because I just loved the house and garden', she says as we begin our stroll. 'It was a complete mess and there was no driveway at all,' she recalls. Despite thick clay soil and a high water table, which causes regular flooding, the borders are sensational. The garden may be in a frost pocket, but Anne has ensured that there's colour all year round.

The elegant drawing room windows look down across a broad terrace to a wide sweep of well-manicured lawn. To the left a rose garden with twisting Yorkstone paths nestles by a black summerhouse. Standard roses draw the eye up but are underplanted with a billowing carpet of aromatic catmint, its silvery leaves and lavender-blue flowers competing with the metallic purple leaves and sage and pink blooms of hardy geraniums. Alliums peek through here and there, their starry seedheads adding a structural element that lasts well into winter. Nearby, the black fleshy leaves of *Aeonium* 'Zwartkop' catch my eye, complementing the wooden walls of the summerhouse behind.

'The roses don't mind the water table and

HOME TRUTHS

Size of garden: 3½ acres

Soil type: Clay

Advice: Understand your space, the soil and your lifestyle. Don't be a slave to your garden. Avoid plants that are going to struggle - why lose money?

Favourite plants: 'I'm crazy about plants especially paeonies, but it seems they don't like me!

neither do viburnums or hostas', advises Anne. Nevertheless, she's added plenty of organic matter to improve the soil. 'I dug in compost, manure and blood, fish and bone – a real cocktail – I've never seen such flowers', she recollects. Beyond the roses, a herbaceous border packed with colourful perennials sweeps towards a large rural-looking pond. The grass is longer here and a bench beneath the nearby trees is a natural spot to relax.

With all the trees chosen for their light canopies, the dappled shade they provide is pleasant on a sunny day. We pause by the pond and look out across a stream to fields beyond. A gap in the trees enhances the view, helping the garden merge effortlessly with the countryside beyond.

Used to the vast swathes of acid woodland which predominates where she lived as a child, she planted trees when she arrived as a reminder of home. Betulas have done well at The Old Rectory, but acers have not. 'It's strange,' remarks Anne, '*Acer palmatum* doesn't like me, but it grows well locally'.

Down by the pond Anne comments on how passing and local wildlife works with the garden. 'Ducks eat the fallen apples and are great at getting rid of slugs. There's mink in the stream and I've seen bats, owls, pheasant and partridge.' On the far bank, an old railway cutting that's little more than a gully provides a lush haven for badgers and is packed with ferns, salix and grasses.

The other main border peaks during summer then becomes a fiery mass of red and orange during autumn. Purple-leaved plants such as *Cotinus coggygria* 'Grace', the cercis 'Forest Pansy', beech, *Berberis ottawensis* 'Superba' and the salix 'Nancy Saunders' give added depth and continuity as you move from one end to the other.

Hellebores also feature highly, giving colour from late winter into spring. The luminescent pale green flowers of *H foetidus* glow in the soft light, while the spiny-leaves of *H argutifolius* create a

The pond is a natural draw for wildlife and, with the odd tidy up, regulates itself

The clay soil has been worked with rather than fought against to create what you see here. It's enlightening

glossy, structural backdrop against which the creamy, purple-pink blooms of *H sternii* can really shine. The cerise, pink and white flowers of *Cyclamen coum* also lighten the shade after Christmas.

Over the years Anne has admired designers such as Robin Lane Fox and Christopher Lloyd. 'I love Sissinghurst and they've done a good job at Hatfield. Prince Charles' garden at Highgrove is great as well'. Rupert Golby (author of 'The Well-Designed Garden') is a regular visitor who constantly makes new suggestions.

'I've got no time for garden makeovers. They just encourage people to want something they can't have. Don't you think it's all too instant? It's not real. There's no hard work involved. Mind you, I'm not the best planner. My borders are more of a concept than a definite plan. But concepts can work, even if there's an element of trial and error'.

One of Anne's first tasks when she moved in was to take out the double borders, clear the pond and create a new veg garden. 'I was a bit disdainful of growing veg', she admits, 'but I called Rosemary Verey, who was a friend of my mother-in-law and she helped with the plans and permanent planting. Anne chose the veg but confesses, 'I was so unsure about crop rotation, I called Thompson & Morgan weekly at one stage'. The potager is now established and Anne's fifteen years of experience combined with that of her gardeners Rob and Susan clearly shows. It's a masterpiece.

Neat box hedges surround colourful beds of vegetables, fruit and herbs. Apples are trained over archways and wire spheres or grown as stepovers to line pathways. Espaliers of fruit clothe the walls. The peaches enjoy the southerly aspect and are protected from the spores that cause peach leaf curl by a glass overhang, which keeps

The sunken rose garden is also home to nepeta, hardy pink geraniums, yuccas and a tub of sempervivums with a fleshy black aeonium in the centre

From the top:
The daisy-like blooms of Helipterum 'Pierrot';
The seedheads of fennel add structure in autumn;
Sunflowers from seed;
A self-seeded Japanese anemone emerges from the rustic path of the potager

From the top:
Swiss chard adds splashes of colour into winter;
Tomatoes ripen in the warm summer sun;
Stepover apple trees make neat edging and yield fruit;
Flowers, fruit and veg in the potager

'At some point you can say a house is finished. I can paint a room yellow and leave it for several years.
But it's not the same in a garden. There's always something that needs doing'.

off the rain. Large terracotta jars for forcing rhubarb are grouped at their base.

Although highly productive, the vegetable garden is planted with beauty in mind. Red-leaved lettuces contrast with feathery clumps of bright green parsley and the silvery purple leaves of cabbage. The strawberry beds are enclosed by small lavender hedges above which the variegated ball-shaped heads of *Salix integra* 'Hakuro-nishiki' add extra height. 'Potagers are great for families', she enthuses, 'children can get involved without walking on the vegetables. I find they love growing sweetcorn, pumpkins and gourds'.

There is a strong design element to the potager. Every pathway leads you onward, to an obelisk, a bench or even a collection of containers. Topiary abounds with domes of box, spheres of euonymus and tightly clipped hedges of *Ilex crenata*. Many of the box plants have been infected by a fungus disease, which started gradually six years ago. The hedges were killed off in the middle so Rupert suggested a dwarf variety of *Ilex crenata*, which has been very effective. 'The disease fools you', says Anne. 'The infected area gets covered by fresh growth and you feel encouraged, but then it rains and gets worse again.'

Anne loves hellebores and these appear frequently in the woodland garden behind the potager. 'I buy a lot from nurseries - hellebores from Ashwoods, paeonies from Kelways and roses from Peter Beales.' There are some choice shrubs as well, such as the almond-scented *Oemleria cerasiformis*, a twisted hazel and a purple-flowered *Daphne mezereum*. In spring a tunnel of wisteria is

The evening light catches the pale, almost chlorotic leaves of *Salix integra* 'Hakuro-nishiki' which stand proud at the back of the potager

another highlight, it's pale purple blooms dangling overhead. Naturalized plantings of narcissi including the delicate *N cyclamineus* with its reflexed petals add splashes of colour underfoot.

Although Anne's garden looks good all year round, her work still isn't complete. 'At some point you can say a house is finished. I can paint a room yellow and leave it for several years. But, it's not the same in a garden. There's always something that needs doing'.

Anne grows hundreds of plants from seed and cuttings, especially salvias, pelargoniums and bedding for her containers. 'Pots are fun. I ring the changes every year because this is in the National Gardens Scheme.'

A large polytunnel gives Susan the room to grow all the annuals they need to keep the garden looking its best for visitors.